Echoes of Communism
Lessons From An American By Choice

Dr. Ileana Johnson Paugh

DEDICATION

I dedicate this book to my Dad, Florin Apostolescu, who allowed me to pursue my dreams in a free country although he knew that he would not see me as often as he wanted. My Dad made the ultimate sacrifice for his anti-communist stance. He is my hero and a Romanian patriot.

My Mom and Dad, the year I left my home

TABLE OF CONTENTS

ACKNOWLEDGMENTS

I want to thank my husband, David Scott Paugh, for encouraging me to write short essays of my struggles to adapt to American culture and my years of growing up in communist Romania.

.

Map of Romania

"Socialism only works in two places: Heaven where they don't need it and Hell where they already have it." Ronald Reagan

INTRODUCTION

When I set foot in America, I always felt that I was being watched. The communists have etched such a huge fear in my heart that I was afraid to tell anyone where I came from, what I experienced, and how I lived. I thought some nefarious secret agent would arrive one day to exact retribution because I abandoned the communist cause that I never embraced in the first place. This fear was not irrational, far-fetched or misplaced. Although I came here legally, I was told by Romanian authorities repeatedly before I left to keep my mouth shut or else.

Many defectors had to hide and assume alter egos for fear of reprisals or death. They were indeed found dead under mysterious circumstances, while the famous had tragic and more bizarre ends. Some were irradiated and died slow painful deaths; others ate poisoned food and died swiftly. Some were injected with toxic chemicals and died quickly as well. Others were tortured, shot, or dismembered, their bodies to be found in strange locations, miles away from their homes.

Police subjected families at home to torture, mistreatment, beatings, and constant harassment. They were refused visas, passports, requests to move to other towns, jobs, admission to college, and promotions, as a form of punishment for the transgressions of their relatives who chose to live free overseas. My father was beaten repeatedly during interrogations because his only daughter chose to live free and marry an American.

Every knock on the door caused me great anxiety; the sight of a police officer or highway patrol officer induced tachycardia and sweat. In my communistic experience, the officers were not working to defend my freedom but to punish, abuse, beat, and incarcerate citizens without any benefit of due process. In Romania, we were guilty until proven innocent. Trumped-up charges would be fabricated overnight and there was nothing we could do to defend ourselves.

The stories I am about to tell, have been swirling inside my head for quite some time. Over the years, I wanted to share my childhood memories and recollections of growing up under communism with my students and friends. I was reluctant to sacrifice my objectivity as a teacher – students were entitled to decide right from wrong without professorial coaxing. There was already quite a bit of indoctrination into the liberal/progressive mindset. American schools were and are a breeding ground for socialist/Marxist professorial agendas. For the life of me, I could not understand why these people called themselves progressives when they were actually regressing the quality of education and the standard of living if they were buying and selling utopian socialism/communism.

Most teachers were proud members of NEA and quite unwelcoming of any conservatives or ideas that deviated from their talking points and ideology. I understood that students might be incredulous for the simple reason that most have not really experienced government-induced hard times, government abuse, serious lack of basic needs, or lack of freedom. How can anybody relate to poverty under communism when there is such an overabundance of everything in America, even for the citizens who are on welfare and consider themselves poor?

The clash of cultures in America was overwhelming at times, I held it all inside and tried to adapt the best I could. The dictum ran in my mind, "when in Rome, do as the Romans do."

I blamed myself for cultural and societal shortcomings; it was my duty to adjust to my new way of life without complaint or sign of discomfort. Discomfort did come from many directions every day, like stray bullets. Few fellow Americans had the capacity or patience to understand uprooting and adaptation problems. There was no room for error, patience, or understanding.

For the most part, I was quite successful. That is not to say that success did not come with a heavy price tag - loss of cultural identity. I mourned the loss of who I was for many years – I was the only Romanian in the State of Mississippi for the longest time, no family, and there was no Internet to communicate far away, quickly, and cheaply. Phone calls were expensive and the connection garbled at best.

There were few other foreigners and we had gatherings from time to time to share our lives and sacrifices with each other – Chinese, Thai, Poles, Russians, Indians, and Iranians. Some came here legally like me and others defected. Nobody jumped a fence or crossed the Rio Grande but every person had an interesting story to tell and we relished our common ground of being outsiders trying to fit in. It was a monumental task but friends made it easier.

Adjusting to America took on a regional flavor. When I was in the south, people thought I was from Connecticut or worse, as they kindly put it, Euro trash. Some thought I spoke German, others Italian. I actually speak both.

The fact that I spoke several foreign languages baffled friends, acquaintances, and neighbors in the south. I felt uncomfortable and it infuriated me when they praised me endlessly as if I was some curiosity at the circus. I knew, however, they were being kind and polite.

After many years of teaching, by the 20th class or so, I was now speaking fourteen languages as opposed to seven. My fame and linguistic attributes increased since most Americans were in awe of people who could speak more than one language. Isolation and a huge land mass, made it unnecessary to speak anything else but English.

Things changed so drastically that I can no longer recognize the country I adopted in 1978. Our American border with Mexico is no longer secured. Millions of illegal aliens crossed into the U.S. over the years and still do, for better economic opportunities. Since we did not and do not have an official language, Spanish has unofficially become our second language. Politicians passed law after law demanding that everything from road signs, health care, directions, phone, driving manuals, voting ballots, education, to packaging be done bilingually – press 2 for Spanish. Americans are now finding themselves in the predicament of having to learn a foreign language in their own country. Anything short of that labels them bigoted and racist.

When I traveled in the northeastern U.S., I was viewed as a southerner. Interlocutors would automatically deduct I.Q. points or dismiss me. I did not have much of an accent but the trace of it and the fact that I spoke proper English all the time made people remark insensitively, "you ain't from around here, are you?" The stereotypes of north vs. south lingered.

The elitist snobs from the northeast had an issue with me as a resident of the south. A group from Boston, who was scheduled to share a bus with us on a trip to Italy, decided to pay for a bus of their own at considerable expense. Their letter requesting the bus explained that their highly educated faculty with master's degrees could not possibly share a bus with us, southern hicks. I promptly replied that I had a Ph.D. in my field of expertise and so did my colleagues. Elitism and ignorance were hard or impossible to eradicate.

Most Americans, who were geographically challenged, had no clue where I came from, where Romania was located on the map. When I explained that it was sandwiched between the former Soviet Union, Bulgaria, Hungary, Yugoslavia, and the Black Sea, the confusion deepened. It was a far-away place that they would never have to travel to, and it was better left unknown.

When I was tired, my "foreignness" became more obvious through subtle or quite embarrassing pronunciation errors. That was because certain sounds of the English language were not natural to a Latin based language as Romanian. It is true, fifty-one percent of our English vocabulary is Latin based, but the pronunciation is definitely Anglo-Saxon. To enunciate correctly, speakers have to make a real effort to place the tongue properly. After a while, the muscles get tired and the authentic accent can suffer. For example, the long "e" in "sheets" became short "e" as in "shits." You can imagine the embarrassing moments when trying to purchase sheets but using the short "e," or telling students on air that they must complete their worksheets and using again the short "e."

When my children were small, they were ashamed of sounding foreign and begged me and grandma to stop speaking Romanian in public. They did not want to be rejected or misunderstood because they appeared to belong to another culture. To be different was perceived as unwelcome in southern society. My children's request not to speak Romanian in public was impossible to accommodate since mom did not speak English at all. Over the years, she tried to learn it repeatedly, but found it impossible to remember the words. Mom could, however, still recite poetry from her childhood.

My girls seldom invited friends to spend the night in our home unless they were children of the military. As they traveled extensively with their families and understood what it felt like to be an outsider, the military culture was much more cosmopolitan and accepting of foreigners.

As my daughters grew older, they began to appreciate the ability to speak Romanian, which set them apart from their monolingual peers. Besides, it made good entertainment to be able to make secret remarks in public. As toddlers, they cornered mom and me on more than one occasion – as we addressed them in Romanian, they responded in English, and very loudly, creating many comical situations.

All the stories of becoming an American citizen, the pride, the pain, the hard work, experiencing good and bad along the way while weaving myself into the fabric of society, being an American longer than I was a Romanian, where I came from, why, and how, needed to be told.

At my husband David's insistence and encouragement, I started a blog, which expanded with each essay.

The blog was born out of frustration with our society's sudden and furious march toward socialism with the election of an ultra-liberal president who was so charismatic and promised utopia to everyone. It rang hollow to me and, at the same time, it reminded me of the communist propaganda that promised everything under the sun and delivered nothing but poverty and misery.

Why were Americans so mesmerized and willing to give up their wonderful lives for an empty promise?

I knew that growing up in a communist society was no walk in the park, certainly not the romantic vision that American teachers have indoctrinated into their students' heads in the last thirty years.

I made speeches on the topic of growing up under communism and many listeners wanted me to help educate young people about the dangers of communism. I decided that my stories must become a book and serve as a lesson that freedom is precious and must be guarded at all costs.

I dedicated this book to my Dad, Florin Apostolescu, who died before he saw freedom from the oppressive communist regime that tortured his mind, soul, and body for 29 years.

These vignettes are glimpses into the universe of a child and a young woman growing up under communism and the pained, tumultuous transition of a young adult to life in a free, capitalist society.

AMERICAN PARADISE - JANUARY 13, 1978

My march to freedom began on a Friday the 13th early in the morning in my parent's concrete slab, government issued apartment, cracked and decaying from lack of maintenance and the 1977 earthquake that had destroyed hundreds of buildings.

I had packed my modest suitcase the week before with my spare pair of shoes, my one dress, favorite books, and my freshly issued Romanian passport.

Many people would have killed to possess it and the blue stamped visa from the American Embassy. My mom had packed another suitcase with hand-sewn sheets that would never fit an American bed, doilies, my wedding dress, and wedding presents from various relatives. I gave my wedding dress away years later so that two other cousins would have a bridal gown. My $700 wedding dress was definitely a wise and generous investment.

I had no money in my pocket; I was going to the land of plenty, who needs money there? We had this vision that money grows on trees in America and all you have to do is reach up and pluck it.

My wedding guests had given my parents gifts of money but they barely covered the cost of the wedding. I did not want my daddy to lose all his life savings for giving me such a beautiful wedding - I gave him all the money. I had no remorse leaving other gifts behind.

I was full of trepidation and anxious to start my new life in America but fear was beginning to grip my heart as I looked pensively at my very few possessions around the room that had been my bedroom, my study, my living room, my library for 19 years. I could not take any of it with me.

Objects did not define me but I wanted to take a small part of my past life with me, to remind me of who I was and were I came from. Most of all, I wanted to take my parents with me - they had worked so hard to make sure I was safe, I loved them with all my heart, and now I was abandoning them.

Uncle John was driving us to the airport in his beat-up Dacia and other relatives were following by bus. It was a relatively short trip, 65 km, but it might as well have been a long drive to the scaffold.

The closer I got to the airport, the more I regretted my decision and doubted my sanity. Will I be able to get on the plane and fly away from everybody and everything I held dear and loved? Who will offer me the warmth and love that had enveloped me for 19 years?

The customs officers were very rude and attempted to confiscate my modest engagement ring. Only wedding bands were permitted to leave the country. There was a shortage of gold and nobody could "export" any gold jewelry unauthorized. Certainly, this thin ring worth maybe $100 had to stay behind. Jean, who had given the ring to me as a family heirloom, was beside herself with outrage. She took the ring away from me and put it on her finger. As an American citizen, she could leave the country with any gold jewelry she wore. Problem solved with a $20 bribe to the custom officer who ignored the ring exchange. I kept this ring for 13 years while I was married to Sam, and had to return it to the Johnson family when our divorce was final.

I felt so lucky to leave the country and cursed at the same time - I was torn between the love for my family and the yearning to be free in America. It was an icy cold January morning but I was trembling from fear and anxiety. Part of me could not wait to go and part of me wished that the plane stalled.

Would my visa be recalled at the last minute? Sam was nervous and irritated with all the communist red tape he had endured for the past year - he was bubbling over with impatience and anger - he felt trapped and imprisoned in this third world country that did not respect any rights a human being had in America. He felt humiliated and emasculated.

I kept hugging everybody and crying in desperation. The plane was taking off late as usual. Nothing was punctual in Romania. I said my last goodbyes to my parents, my uncles, my aunts, and my cousins. It felt more like a funeral, with all the tears and constant hugs. I did not know it yet, but my life would be fundamentally transformed in a way that I had never envisioned.

I had no idea the amount of pain I had caused my loved ones and the longing and suffering my parents and I will experience for years to come. Was it selfishness of a typical teenager or the ignorance of a young person eager to spread her wings and fly away, so far away that she would never be able to come back? I was just happy to get out, to be free. Was it a pyrrhic victory? What was the cost of freedom for me? I left part of my heart behind on that frigid January.

Last Photo of Ileana before leaving Romania

ARRIVAL IN NEW YORK

The flight was long and amazing. Everything around me was a source of wonder. I felt like a princess when the stewardess would cater to my every whim - in 1978, flying was a real class act, people actually dressed up to fly and were treated with respect, not condescension as it is often the case today.

The food was exquisite and served with stainless steel silverware, real napkins, glasses, and marvelous little containers filled with food. I did not have to stand in line to be told often times at the head of the line, "sorry, we just ran out, come back tomorrow."

I could not believe my eyes! I looked around with fear, wondering when the police would come to pull us off the flight or ask for our papers. Nobody left home without forms of identification, especially the official communist I.D. that everyone received upon turning 14, the age of consent. This I.D. was the size of a small passport with stamps indicating various address moves, criminal offenses, or traffic violations.

Uncle Nelu had managed to bribe one of the border guards with a carton of Kent cigarettes and a crisp $20 bill so I can keep the modest diamond ring that Jean had given me.

Cigarettes were desired commodity money during communist Romania, along with soap, shampoo, chocolate, pantyhose, and makeup. The most popular brands of cigarettes were Kent and Chesterfield. Twenty dollars bought a whole carton. Some services required bribes of just one package of Kent, others an entire carton. This bribe required more since it involved keeping our own property, a $100 gold ring. Visits to doctors, lab work, and other medical interventions required both bribes of money and commodity money.

Twenty-four hours later and after stopover in Hungary and Germany, we arrived in New York. I was penniless, hungry, thirsty, bewildered, tired, and apprehensive.

What have I done? Where was I? Who were all these people? Will I be able to survive on my own? I have no money, no home, no job, no family, and no friends. I wanted to run back home to my family and everything that was familiar and made me happy. Separated by a vast ocean, I was 8,000 miles away. I did not even have 10 cents in my pocket to buy a soda or make a phone call.

Jane and Sam were my salvation now and I was clinging to them for dear life. After going through customs and having my meager belongings rifled through, we boarded another flight bound for Mississippi.

I watched in horror as the lights started to disappear and all I could think of was, where is the city, where are the lights? I grew up in the city of Ploiesti, over 650,000 inhabitants and I was moving to a town with a little over 3,000 citizens.

We landed in Memphis were we boarded yet another flight to Golden Triangle Regional Airport (GTR), a small local airport servicing three adjacent small towns, located in the middle of cow pastures.

I was totally depressed and crying by now, doubting my sanity and wishing that I had listened to my Daddy who had tried valiantly to warn me that I should not go with such high expectations to a strange country and state that I knew nothing about.

He said that my high expectations might turn out to be a big disappointment. How was I to know that I would leave a third world communist country and trade it in for a developed republic with agricultural, Deep South flavor?

Once we landed at the regional airport in the middle of a single runway, I collected my luggage from the belly of the Republic airplane. We finally embarked on a two-hour drive through lone highways to the Johnson farm in Sparta, MS.

The ranch house was modern and luxurious by any Romanian standards, with indoor plumbing, running water, flushable toilettes, electricity, and lots of space. Jane's closet was as big as our kitchen. The darkness was scary but the soothing sounds of farm animals were calming.

Mr. Johnson did not say a word and offered everyone hot chocolate except me. I was too bewildered to care or even have an opinion. I was finally in the land of opportunity, free of communist oppression, and all I wanted to do was to go back home to my poverty and my family.

Ileana in Sparta,, MS

MY NEW HOME IN SPARTA

I was too excited, scared, and anxious to sleep. Every object, smell, landscape looked utterly unfamiliar and scary. I did not know how to act; the English I learned in school did not resemble at all the Southern slang I was hearing. I had to ask Sam to explain to me what people said all the time.

I felt lonely, isolated, and did not trust anything or anybody. I was expecting a knock on the door any moment to take me away to jail. Every time I saw a police officer, sheriff, or a state trooper my heart would race and I fully expected them to ask me for my papers.

I was finally free from communism but did not understand anything around me. I needed time to explore my newfound freedom. The problem was that this newfound freedom was in the middle of a cow pasture, ten miles away from the nearest hamlet, I had no car, and did not know how to drive. Women were not encouraged to drive in Romania and we were certainly too poor to own a car.

I could not understand why the population could come and go as they wished without the government giving them permission and without legally notarized papers , why they could move from town to town, state to state, change jobs, own property, or do anything for that matter. Surely, there must have been some centralized power that pulled the strings to make this society run so smoothly. My understanding of how capitalism ran so successfully without any centralized interference was minimal.

The next morning the constant parade of visitors began - I was a novelty, almost like a new circus act in town that everybody had to come gawk at, touch, and ask question of, marveling at my foreign accent and my "exotic" looks. If I had to hear the word exotic one more time, I was going to explode.

People would ask stupid and insensitive questions out of sheer ignorance. "Do they take a bath in Romania?" "Sure, once a month, whether we need it or not." I felt compelled at first to answer the idiotic questions truthfully, but, after a while, it got old, and I had to improvise by being sarcastic or cocky. I had as much fun with it as I was legally allowed to do so. "Do women drive in Romania?" Not really, we still use wagons with oxen." That was not so far from the truth in country areas where people were still backwards, riding wagons with wheels made of car tires, pulled by horses.

I was fascinated by the fact that even the most remote farms in the boondocks had plumbing and indoor bathrooms. That was so unbelievable to me; the septic tank was a novelty since my grandparents and the family at large that lived in rural areas still used a hole in the ground covered with wooden slats, good luck trying not to fall in the big goo of poop.

I still remember my grandparents' water source - a hand pump that resembled the 1900s water pumps. In fact, my paternal grandmother took her drinking water from a well about two miles up the mountain. It was fun coming down, but way too difficult climbing with a big wooden bar over your shoulders, balancing two heavy buckets, one on each end.

Has anybody seen a bathtub or shower in the country? Not really. My maternal grandfather, ever the enterprising engineer, had rigged a rusted bucket over the outhouse for impromptu showers when the August sun was strong enough to warm the water. We would pull a string, tilt the bucket, and the entire content would rinse the pre-soaped body. That was our shower.

Did we take showers in winter? They still had Turkish baths in the city. Villagers could bathe occasionally for a meager fee - the interior looked positively medieval, dank, dingy, dirty, dark, and quite smelly. It was always frightening to go with my mother when the communist government would cut our hot water off in the city in summer time or cut water off period for reasons of rationing. The official excuse was that they had to clean the large vat of mineral deposits. This process took three to four months each summer.

You can imagine how spoiled and privileged I felt in the backwoods of Mississippi having a hot shower, running water, and an indoor commode. I felt positively rich. Gone were the summers when we pooped in the cornfields because the outhouse stunk. Grandpa always lectured us on the bacterial sins of befouling the corn crops. The corn looked greener and healthier to me and it tasted even better.

The next major outing with my new family was going to the Baptist Church in Mantee. I did not know what to expect since my mother-in-law believed I was pagan on account of my orthodox religion.

She considered our marriage on January 7, 1978 in St. John's Romanian Orthodox Cathedral with four priests non-existent since it was not performed in the Baptist Church. The marriage took place in Ploiesti, Romania, with almost 200 friends and family in attendance. Never mind that the Orthodox Church was one of the oldest religions in the world, she insisted that we had to marry again, otherwise our children would be bastards.

I learned not to object much so as not to raise the ire of my new in-laws. I agreed with her, or pretended to, but I did what I thought was the proper thing to do as an orthodox Christian.

The most ardent defender of my new status was Tom, Mr. Johnson's hired hand. He had a heart of gold but was poor as a church mouse. I could never understand what he said, I would have needed a dictionary for that because he spoke in slang. He was pretty much toothless on account of his smoking habits, but he did teach me a few choice idiomatic expressions. Tom introduced me to wild game, especially fried snapping turtle from one of the farm's many ponds - it tasted like chicken.

MY FIRST TRIP TO THE GROCERY STORE

Europeans are used to shopping for food on a daily basis. Italians, French, Germans like their bread, vegetables and meats very fresh. They shop in small quantities and do not like to refrigerate or freeze their food. One of the reasons may be that their living space and refrigerators are small and it is not part of their culture to freeze food.

For us, Eastern Europeans, it was not just a matter of apartments being small, many families did not own, or could not afford a refrigerator. Nobody even knew that freezers existed.

Our refrigerator in wintertime was the window ledge in the kitchen. In summer time, we chilled bottles and watermelons in the tub. The tub was not used anyway since we did not have hot water in the summer. In wintertime, the birds got clever and realized that we stored food on the window ledge and made pecking runs.

Families, who could afford a refrigerator, had a hard time paying for electricity or had ruined food from the daily blackouts. Rationing of electricity was a common theme.

Even western Europeans had issues with electricity - you could not run the drier and the microwave at the same time without causing a total shutdown of electricity for the entire complex of apartments. While in Italy, I often short-circuited the entire network while drying clothes and making tea in the microwave at the same time.

My Dad often joked that the reason we did not own a fridge was the lack of food to put in it. He was right, but price was an issue too. It cost the salary for 3-4 months of an average worker. Few people could save enough money to buy a fridge with cash, there was no such thing as buying on credit.

Shopping or food was an endless line for bones, wilted or rotten veggies, and basic staples if you had enough rationing coupons.

Every family was issued a limited amount of rationing coupons that looked like fiscal stamps - we clipped them for rice, sugar, cooking oil, butter, milk, flour, etc. Each family was entitled to one kilogram of each per month, about 2 pounds. Once we ran out of rationing coupons, even though we had money to buy, nobody would sell unless we had coupons.

This created a thriving black market full of cheats, stealing from work, bartering what they stole for something else stolen that was in short supply, thus enabling people to survive. If you worked in a wine factory, you would trade stolen bottles of wine with a butcher who stole meat from the state run butcher shop, etc.

Black market racketeers, who would steal rationing coupons, would sell food bought in stores for ten times the price they paid. The ruling elite was insulated from such practices or from standing in 3-4 hour lines for bananas, toilet paper, or whatever one needed because they had their own private stores where ordinary citizens were not allowed to enter or shop.

As for my family, I was glad when we could find even shriveled potatoes because it meant sustenance as opposed to starvation.

I was often sad when I came back from school and I could not even find shriveled potatoes to bake or make fries. We did not have school breakfasts or lunches, if we ate anything during school, we brought from home.

Food was scarce in general and I did not know of any obese people, we were all underweight and not necessarily healthy.

Fruits and veggies were only sold in season. Sometimes in winter time my dad would disappear all day and bring home some shriveled grapes, almost raisins, a few dry apples, or fruit compote, and he had this wonderful grin on his face that he could bring his little girl a special treat when she was sick with the flu or bronchitis. I adored my dad and fully appreciated the sacrifices he had to make in order to feed us.

The food lines usually stretched for a mile or two, winding around the blocks. It was common occurrence for people passing by to join a line before they even knew what the store was selling. We knew instinctively that, whatever it was, toilet paper, soap, cooking oil, shampoo, vitamins, cotton, we needed it.

Everyone was in stock up mode, carried collapsible shopping bags, and lots of cash in case the need arose. People were robbed often since writing checks or credit cards did not exist in a communist regime.

One central bank allowed citizens to have savings accounts or specialized accounts for purchasing cars but no checking accounts. It took years for car deliveries and the customers had to have the entire amount in a car savings account before they could register their name on the production/purchase list.

My first grocery trip was at Horn's Big Star in Houston, MS. This was certainly not a supermarket since the town of Houston only had 3,000 inhabitants and a little over 50,000 people in the county. However, to me, it might as well have been Harrods's of London or Galleries Lafayette in Paris.

I was speechless at the rows and rows of packaged, frozen, and fresh food. The bright light was dazzling, the polite staff, the immaculate floors, shelves, and the lack of lines were stunning.

Sam was laughing at my shocked demeanor - I could not fathom where all this fresh food had come from. The packaging was so colorful and beautiful; it looked like a work of art to me.

I was filling my grocery cart as if there was going to be a 50 year famine. I did not know what to choose, I felt like a child in a candy store with a myriad of choices. I could picture myself as a chicken who, when presented with an endless supply of food, gorged so much that it eventually died of overeating.

I became Horn's Big Star frequent customer, relishing in the ability to buy fresh fruit any time I wanted. The apples were plump and fresh, coming in many varieties, ruby red, yellow, green, rosy, sweet, tart, etc. No more shriveled up or wormy fruits in summer time. I could eat apples or any fruits year round.

I felt the luckiest girl in the world! I had tears in my eyes and I still do when I think of the experience and how I was explaining it to my Mom and Dad on the phone. To say that they were incredulous is an understatement. Only in heaven would people have such an abundance of food, endless rows of choices, cheap prices, attractive packaging, and free samples to boot. What a blessed country!

Americans do not really appreciate the fact that they only spend 15% of their incomes on food, the store shelves are plentiful, and there is a nearby store open 24/7 in case they run out of food in the middle of the night. Americans don't' know that other cultures spend most of their days working to earn enough money for food.

MY FIRST TRIP TO THE HOSPITAL

My husband Sam and I drove to Tupelo in his grandfather's old beat up 1962 Chevrolet Impala. I learned how to drive in this car around the pastures on the farm in Woodland, terrorizing poor cows. It was the color of puke green and the seats had seen better days, oozing rubber from every vinyl crack. It baked in the sun while Sterling went fishing.

We were glad to have the old car, it was heavy, solid metal and chrome everywhere, burned a quart of oil a week, but it always cranked and took us where we needed to go. I covered the seats with towels, to make it more comfortable to ride in. When we went to parties or church, people were too embarrassed to ride with us. I was happy that we had wheels!

My in-laws had decided that I should take my tonsils out. They were giving me quite a bit of trouble in this new climate. I was scared to death since I have never been admitted to a hospital before and I did not know what to expect, especially in a foreign country.

I had heard horror stories under communist care and I saw the results of Romanian surgical skills hopping on crutches, deformed, maimed, or worse, in graves. I was frightened and I knew, I was going to die. I had no clue that I would be the beneficiary of the best health care system in the world.

I have had issues with tonsil infections growing up. I was given so much Streptomycin in Romania, I am still surprised that I can see, hear, and smell.

Moving to a very different climate, a sub-tropical, extremely humid and hot, created challenges that my body was unable to fight off very well and exacerbated any symptom I have previously had.

I was plagued by more infections and severe nose bleeds from allergies to plants and flowers indigenous to Mississippi but unknown to my immune system.

I was born and raised in a temperate continental climate and my body was rebelling against the oppressively hot and humid sub-tropical climate of this southern state. When I walked outside, it felt like an oven was sucking the breath out of me.

On our way to the clinic in Tupelo, I felt like going to the scaffold. I had asked my husband for a last meal at KFC, it was the only food that somewhat resembled the fried chicken I ate in Romania, and, if I was going to die, I wanted to have comfort food as my last supper. He refused, since surgical patients could not eat and drink hours before surgery.

We did have insurance, it was quite expensive for newlyweds, $200 or so per month in 1978 dollars, but we wanted to be responsible Americans and were not expecting a handout from anybody. I think our combined income at the time was $600 per month and we lived with our in-laws. That did not leave us much disposable income.

The clinic was like a luxury hotel. The friendliness of the admission personnel and staff in general was a sharp contrast to the insulting rudeness and carelessness of the Romanian medical corps.

The bed was clean, comfortable, I did not have to bring my own sheets, I had my own room, nurses checked on me every so many minutes, the doctors were friendly, knowledgeable, and did not reuse needles and bandages.

I had my own bathroom in the room, I had a TV, and the walls had been freshly painted in a "cheerful" grey color. Even so, it beat the Romanian hospitals where layers of paint from World War II were still chipping everywhere, revealing water, rust, and bloodstains. The floor in this beautiful hospital was spotless and shiny, not a mosaic of dubious stains. Beautiful paintings cheered the rooms and hallways.

Imagine that, a TV in my hospital room - I had to wait until twelfth grade in high school in order to have a black and white TV in my home with two channels playing mostly communist propaganda.

It was lunchtime in the clinic, the aroma of cooked food was everywhere, and I thought, "Great, I might get to have my last meal after all." At least my family did not have to cook it and bring it to me to the hospital. We had to cook Dad's and Grandpa's meals every day and trek them across the city to the hospital in Romania, otherwise they starved.

Slightly drowsy and confused from Demerol, feeling no pain, I thought I had died and went to heaven and I just did not know it yet. I gave my husband my last wishes before they put me to sleep, firmly believing that I would not wake up again as I was counting backwards from 10.

I had written a good-bye letter to my parents. In typical independent young person fashion, I had not told them I was having surgery - I did not want them to worry unnecessarily - there was nothing they could have done since I was 8,000 miles away.

I woke up in the recovery room, fire in my throat, and I thought, "Oh, I did not go to heaven, I must be in hell and it hurts so badly." There were some angelic faces in a bright light telling me to wake up, the surgery is over.

I closed my eyes and wished it all to go away. I spied a beautiful bouquet of flowers next to my bed, sent by my friend Lois, and I really thought I had died. However, every time I swallowed my saliva, a volcanic burn enveloped my throat.

I asked for water and they brought me ice. I was shocked since I remembered my little cousin Rodica having the same surgery and being given hot tea. I was offered ice, ice cream, and slimy jello. Rodica was in misery for weeks, it was probably the hot tea causing her slow and painful recovery. I was pondering my demise from so much burning pain but ice cream was truly a miraculous cure.

Romanians and Europeans in general have this fixation with cold drinks causing sore throat and stomach cramps. That is why everything served there is room temperature. Waiters give customers dirty looks if they ask for ice and bring demonstratively only a cube or two. A doctor performing a tonsillectomy there would never give ice or ice cream to a patient - not when I was growing up.

There were no complications and they sent me home the next day. I called my parents to tell them about my brief encounter with the American medical care. They were incredulous about my descriptions - they thought I was fantasizing and delirious from my surgery and describing an expensive hotel.

Until my Mom saw the inside of an American hospital with her own eyes, she never believed me. To this day, she says that American medicine is very advanced and futuristic, while socialized medical care standards in Romania still need fifty years to catch up.

My grandmother, Elena Cristache, shortly before her death

COMMUNIST MEDICAL CARE

Rationing of everything was a staple of daily life in Romania. We could only have so much before we turned into bourgeois society and we had to be kept under control by the dreaded financial police.

Nobody was allowed to get ahead in any way. If there were appearances that a family had acquired something extra, the neighborhood spies would report them to the economic police. What would these neighborhood spies get in return for their service? Usually the right to shop at the communist party stores, with no lines, better food, more variety, better service, and $150 per month stipend.

Once the police started the investigation, the family had to prove where and how they obtained the money to buy certain things, usually in excess of the identical salaries, barely scraping by, people earned. This was by design to satisfy the utopian communist ideal that everybody had to be equal except the oligarchy in power. Citizens had to prove to the economic police that their "excess" goods were not obtained illegally. You were basically guilty until proven innocent. People hid from their neighbors behind tall fences or wrapped their purchases in newspapers to fend them from prying eyes.

The elites earned more money, were given yearly bonuses, shopped at their own stores, had their own doctors, hospitals, hotels, overseas vacations, Swiss bank accounts, and vacations at national summer resorts with five star hotels and maid service.

Elite beneficiaries of such luxuries bemoaned the societal change in December 1989 from communism to capitalism because they lost all the perks that were unavailable to the proletariat, the unwashed masses.

Everyone lived in the same drab, concrete block apartments, the size of a studio apartment in the west. Often two families had to share a two-bedroom apartment with only one kitchen and one bathroom.

The Spartan conditions extended to medical care as well. By definition, everything was free. Proper health care was more costly than most families earned. There were bribes to see the doctor, bribes to see the nurse, bribes to see the pharmacist, the lab and X-ray technicians. There were bribes for the janitor when the patient was in the hospital. A family member had to stay with the patient 24/7 and take care of everything, otherwise the patient was not fed, changed, attended to when in distress, bandages changed, etc. The family had to wash the bandages, which were reused numerous times, provide meds, clean needles, and syringes.

The doctor and the nurse sometimes did not show up for days. A patient would be hospitalized for weeks and would not see a doctor almost the entire time unless bribes were offered: bottles of wine, money, foreign chocolate, foreign cigarettes, stockings, shampoo, foreign soap, U.S. dollars, and jewelry.

Doctors and nurses made the same low salaries as any workers and compensated their pay by violating the Hippocratic Oath and refusing to treat someone unless bribes were given.

The quality of doctors and nurses was very questionable since medical school graduates had no practical experience on patients whatsoever only theoretical knowledge. Medical school took six years to complete with no residency requirements.

Most patients took their lives into their own hands when they agreed to have elective surgery. When an emergency arose, the outcome was mostly dire. Even simple operations ended in disaster, nipped colons during appendectomies, nipped voice boxes during thyroidectomy, cut blood vessels, ruptured and nicked organs, etc.

There was no ethical or moral accountability for the death of any human being. Life was worth zero and nobody punished any doctor for malpractice. They were all working for the government, who was the family going to sue for the death of their loved one? How could they possibly sue their own government? Had they tried, they were sure to lose every time.

The sanitary conditions were horrible. Bandages were washed, rewashed, and reused, needles were boiled in rusty metal pans and so were the glass and metal syringes. Nothing was disposable and nothing was autoclaved.

When I was in high school, the entire school received injections with the same three needles and syringes. Every morning they were boiled in a pan and the same were used all day until the next morning when they were boiled again. I do mean boiled, they were not autoclaved. I was lucky because my last name started with A so I was the first to get any shots. The rest of my schoolmates had gotten hepatitis from dirty needles. We were extremely lucky that there was no HIV epidemic yet.

The hospital wards were very dirty and in bad need of repairs and painting. Each ward had twenty to thirty metal beds with mattresses stained with blood and other bodily fluids from endless patients who had used the hospitals.

The family had to bring sheets and blankets for the patient. The floors were not usually mopped and caked blood and other stains were present.

Food was not provided by the hospital and family members had to take turns to bring nourishment and water to the patient every day. No IV fluids were provided.

Each hospital had one ambulance that was equipped with nothing to save lives and did not have an EMT on duty. A driver would supplement his salary on the way to an emergency by giving rides to hitchhikers. Most ambulances arrived too late to save someone's life. However, if the patient had non-life threatening emergency, they were lucky to survive the long, uncomfortable, and arduous trip to the hospital in an empty ambulance on the bumpy roads.

Dental care was non-existent. Nobody was allowed to clean his or her teeth at the dentist; it was too expensive and too capitalist. I am not even sure dentists knew how to do that or had the proper equipment to clean teeth.

The only time we were allowed to make an appointment, if we were lucky, was when someone needed teeth pulled or a root canal. I still remember the dentist who talked and spit in my mouth when I was 15. He was doing a root canal without any anesthetic, oblivious to my screams of pain and the dripping blood on my clothes. He had nicked the inside of my mouth with the drill.

The treatment was stretched over a period of three months. I cannot begin to tell you the pain that this man subjected me to unnecessarily. People tried to avoid the dentist like the plague and did their best to brush their teeth if they could find toothbrushes and toothpaste. Both items were in constant shortage.

There were no such things as tampons or pads. Women had to use rags from old clothes or purchase bags of folded cotton, which was also very hard to find at the pharmacy.

Pharmacies compounded most drugs if they had the ingredients. Few drugs were already pre-made in pill form or pre-measured glass vials. These glass vials could be cut with a file and the bitter content swallowed, or it could be injected. Chemicals in powder form had to be mixed with water in a pharmaceutical suspension or the powder was compounded into large paper capsules the size of horse pills, very difficult to swallow.

Meds were always in short supply and people had to bribe pharmacists even for vitamins although technically, they were free. When medicine was available, people did not need prescriptions, they could get whatever drugs they thought might cure their pain.

Birth control pills were not available for sale and were strictly forbidden. Some women managed to purchase a monthly pack from the foreign black market but had no idea how to use them, taking one pill once in a while, thus rendering them ineffective.

There was no such thing as a controlled substance. The government did not care what people ingested, whether people lived or died. We were all considered a burden on society and the few they had to care for medically, the better. We were only valuable as free labor in the fields doing compulsory "volunteer" work.

The government did care about the number of babies born. Because people died at such a young age due to poor nutrition, hard life in general, and lack of proper medical care, the replacement value of the population was not there. There were more people deceased than there were babies born.

Ceausescu's regime decided to reward motherhood with stipends per live born baby and, at the same time, forbade any abortion, period. It became a felony for both the patient and the doctor if a pregnancy ended in abortion, whether it was a spontaneous one or a medically induced one.

If people could not afford the newborn, the government gladly took them and placed them in state orphanages where they were promptly neglected and barely cared for as human beings. So many infants were not cradled or loved by nurses that they became detached and autistic, rocking themselves endlessly.

Women who were raped resorted to back alley abortions and lost their lives. If they survived somehow, the law forbade medical personnel to administer any treatment for infection or blood loss, and the women were given jail sentences.

My maternal grandfather and grandmother were victims of the lack of proper medical care. My grandfather had surgery to repair a hernia and they nicked his colon - he died of gangrene in horrendous pain.

My grandmother had an ulcer and the village doctor gave her aspirin for pain. She bled to death. Neither the surgeon nor the doctor were held accountable for malpractice. After all, they worked for the government.

My best friend had a tonsillectomy and the doctor accidentally nicked her voice box - her voice was never the same, she talked like a chain smoker with a bad case of sore throat.

My Dad, Florin Apostolescu, one year before his death

IN MEMORIAM FLORIN APOSTOLESCU

My Dad, Florin, and Aunt Stela, my godmother, were also victims of communism and its lack of care and value for human beings. Dad passed away on May 12, 1989 and Aunt Stela on May 29, 2010. Dad was 61 years young and Aunt Stela was 76. Both had an unbelievable zest for life. Neither one of them died peacefully, either neglected by the socialized medical bureaucracy or because of anti-communist views.

My biggest regret in life was leaving my family behind and moving to the United States in search of freedom. Nobody could ever accept me in the fold of his or her families like my own family.

I had a very extensive family, 27 first cousins, 14 aunts and uncles, and numerous nieces and nephews whose count I have lost. Eight thousand miles is a long way to stray from everything you have ever known and loved. If anybody got sick or died, we were there within driving or walking distance to give assistance, comfort, help, shelter, food, money, our time, and most important of all, our love.

I lost this connection when I moved to Mississippi, it was severed suddenly and forever like an amputated limb. The phantom pain was indescribably desolate. It was like death without closure. The pain was and is so raw that it makes my throat tighten and cannot breathe.

What do you say to people when they ask, where is your family, where are you going for Christmas, where are you going for Easter? I suddenly became nobody's child, although my parents were still alive.

The guilt I felt was unbearable. If people got sick, I was not there. If people died, I was not there. If people got married, gave birth, baptized their children, I could not be there. It took 24 hours to fly from my home in the United States to my dad's home in Romania.

The plane ticket cost thousands of dollars and talking on the phone was very expensive. Until early 1990s, it cost $3/min or more to talk to Romania, money that I could ill afford. The phone connection took 24 hours sometimes since it was not done through satellites, it was through oceanic cable, and I had to contact the operator, give her the number and wait at home for hours until she could connect me with Romania. The call sounded garbled, as if we were talking underwater. It could cut off at any time and the communist regime always recorded our conversations so we had to be very careful what we said. They always mistreated those left behind.

I was frustrated when people got sick, needed simple drugs or operations that were routine here but life ending over there since surgeons lacked the skills or the equipment to perform them.

I felt guilty that I lived in such a land of plenty yet I could not make a difference in my relatives' lives. I sent them clothes, toys, shoes, aspirin, Tylenol, coloring books, pencils, mittens, scarves, chocolate, children's books, endless packages, but I was helpless with medicine. They could not understand our prescription system, how expensive drugs were, and how desperately poor I was. I could hardly afford care for my children and myself.

When Daddy became partially paralyzed from the cracked skull, after being pushed by his colleagues from a refinery platform, nobody tended to him from Saturday to Wednesday. He languished half-paralyzed until his sister came to visit and found him in such condition. She called the ambulance, which arrived three hours late with no medical help.

He was taken to the hospital where they did precious nothing for him other than let him die a slow and painful death of starvation and thirst. His sister was there to help him eat and drink some but, after a while, he was unable to swallow. The hospital gave him no IV fluids, treatment, or care. He survived for several days because my aunt Marcella kept him alive.

Before and after my Dad passed away, I was not able to fly because I had fractured a disk and I was in traction myself in the hospital. I had no family to care for me, but I had skilled doctors and nurses. I was lucky that mom was here and took care of my little girls.

While in traction, I was agonizing and screaming on the inside that I could not be with my dad. He was on his deathbed and I could not say good-bye. I talked on the phone with doctors whenever I could find one; they were very dismissive, impolite, and uncaring. They had written my Dad off and administered no treatment. I offered to pay anything they wanted in dollars but their skills were not up to the task.

There was only one CT scanner in the country and it was at the military hospital in another town 35 miles away. Dad was not allowed in this facility as it was reserved for the top brass and the ruling elite. Treatment here was out of the question for ordinary citizens.

I spent thousands of dollars on phone calls; talking to people I did not even know, unable to say good-bye to my Dad who, by now, could only speak in whispers. They told me that aunt Marcella pulled his bed to a phone in the ward's hallway, and he heard my voice, tears streaming down his face, but could not talk back.

He died with a wadded picture in his hand of me and his granddaughters in Easter outfits that I had sent him a month earlier. Before he lost his voice, he was telling the doctors how proud he was of his only child who became a doctor in America.

Both families took over and gave my Dad a memorable funeral in the village in which he was born. He was buried next to his mother, the beautiful blue-eyed Ecaterina Apostolescu, who had raised 8 children alone since the age of thirty-two. My paternal grandfather and his brothers had died either in World War II or from wounds acquired in the war.

The extended family on both sides was present at the funeral, yet, here I was, eight thousand miles away in traction from a crushed disk. I felt like the worst child in the world and to this day, I cannot forgive myself for having left my country in spite of the fact that I have raised a family of my own and have made a difference in thousands of students' lives here in the U.S. The fact that I was not there was and is inexcusable.

I was devastated and did not wish to participate in the graduation ceremonies that month at MSU. I was receiving my doctoral degree and President George Bush Sr. was coming to deliver the commencement address.

Doctoral candidates were awarded diplomas directly by the commencement speaker. Their names and field of expertise were announced. Students walked on stage while the President shook their hands. The President of MSU was a jogging friend. He felt sorry for my situation and talked me into attending the Commencement Ceremonies. With tears in my eyes and sorrow in my heart, I walked across the stage and accepted my diploma in my Dad's memory. I later received a letter of condolences from the President of the United States, George Bush Sr.

My Dad was always my inspiration and my role model. I loved his infectious laughter, his broad smile, his dry wit, and his self-deprecating humor. I adored our story time! He was a superb chess master who could play for 8 hours continuously. He loved to go on long walks, was a sharp dresser, and exhibited the curiosity of a cat.

I dedicated all my degrees to my Dad. My mortarboard read, "4 my Dad." I could not have been here without my Dad giving up the only child he has ever had, knowing that he would not see me much anymore, yet proud of who I have become. The communists tortured him by not allowing him to come visit me at all; they declined his visa time after time. I am who I am because of his constant care, sacrifice, love, hard work, and nurturing. I am daddy's girl forever.

Every time I see flowers or my husband David brings me flowers, I think of my Dad, of all the wonderful things he gave up so that I, my children, and all the other people I have touched in my life could have brighter days. In remembrance of him and his name, we celebrate the holiday of flowers, Florii, around the orthodox Easter.

Aunt Stela was mom's middle sister, a skilled accountant, tailor, homemaker, and mother. I spent many years growing up in her home. She held me in church during my baptism as a baby and she was to take over, should something bad had befallen my mother.

She was an inspiration for her tenacity and audacity to do the impossible. She never gave up and had a strong love of learning. She wrote many letters encouraging me to succeed here in the U.S.

As early as last year, at the age of 75, she was strong enough to grow a garden, take care of her two grandchildren, and be a deputy on the village board.

When cancer was discovered on her colon, doctors told her that due to her advanced age, it would be futile for the state to spend so much money to treat her when her life expectancy was fast approaching. Medical resources were limited and had to be rationed under the socialized medical system.

She refused to give up and her youngest son went to work in Italy to earn enough money to pay for her chemotherapy. She underwent treatment but it was too late, the cancer had metastasized to other organs and bones.

She never believed she was going to die, her attitude was positive although she was not receiving enough morphine for pain. I talked to her a lot on the phone during the last months of her life and her positive outlook made me understand that we should not allow pain and despair to rule us.

Life is too short to mourn perennially, it is meant to rejoice and laugh often. Aunt Stela, as her Latin name says, was a true "star," shining brightly now in heaven.

My beloved Dad and Aunt, rest in peace, you will never be forgotten!

FUNERAL FOR STELA

Tuesday, June 1, 2010, Aunt Stela was laid to rest. It was an ominous day with frightening lightning and thunderclaps. The clouds erupted into a torrential rain about the time her coffin was carried outside the home she built with her husband Costel forty years ago.

Romanians are superstitious people, a remnant of the Roman culture. They believe that if it rains, the deceased did not wish to die. If that is true, aunt Stela was the cover story of a spirited woman who wanted to live in spite of her dire circumstances. She believed and hoped for a cure from God until her last breath.

The elders of the village and relatives showed up to celebrate the life of the deceased however, the frightening weather kept many at home.

Stela's wishes were not honored as the government denied permits to build an underground mausoleum. In traditional Roman fashion, she had saved her money in preparation for this day and for a mauseoleum.

Sadly, she had to be buried in a hole in the ground half filled with water. Her casket was huge, as her limbs had separated from joints. She suffered so many fractures, the doctors did not bother to cast them. The bone cancer had eaten up her entire body but not her spirit. She used to tell me that she felt the cancer eating away at her bones.

She was never at peace about death - she did not believe in the afterlife and there was so much to do around the house and garden. She always raised roses and a vegetable garden. She spoke of her roses that needed pruning and love, days before her death.

The village priest tried in vain to bring her peace through numerous confessions but admitted to have failed. She was a tortured soul.

After burial, it was customary to give away food and clothing in memory of the deceased. There were few people left in the hard driving rain to accept these gifts. I know she would have been disappointed as she was a very generous soul.

I wonder what would have happened if the socialist government had been merciful to Stela and not refused her surgery and treatment when she needed it.

Were the people on the death panel responsible for the decision to withhold timely surgery, chemo, and radiation feeling guilty for killing Stela and so many other patients before their time?

Did older people not pay their dues to society? Did they not deserve respect and care in their old age? Did the members of the death panels feel pangs of regret for denying adequate morphine doses to patients who suffered so much pain, they no longer felt human and welcomed death as a relief?

Who but God has the right to make or take life? Is there such a thing as a Hippocratic Oath anymore? Have we become so calloused in the face of pain and suffering? What are we if we cannot be defined by our humanity? Does rationing of medical care through mathematically clever formulas describe how advanced we are technologically, but how low we have sunk ethically and morally?

Aunt Stela was in a coma for ten days with lucid moments among many delirious rants. She was whispering in the last two days of her life. Her last wish was that the priests not spray her body with red wine during the last rites. She did not want to be buried dirty and soiled. She desired to be pretty, makeup in place, just the way she was in life.

I cry for her soul, I hope she found peace. I want to remember her the way she was - full of life, dry and witty humor, and positive until the very end. I spoke with her three weeks before her death and she was actually laughing. What a positively powerful woman! God rest her soul!

Stela, Nicuta, and Monica at her baptism

THE BELLS TOLL FOR NICUTA

Forty years ago, Aunt Nicuta found a two-month-old baby semi-abandoned on a concrete slab at the farmer's market. It was late October, harvest time for grapes, apples, pears, quinces, and plums. The farmer's markets were in full swing. She was swaddled in a dirty blanket that had seen better days. The stench of urine was overpowering - the cloth diapers must have been soaked.

Nicuta asked about the baby's mother and an elderly man pointed to a young, pregnant peasant woman who was selling apples. She asked her gently about the name of the baby who was wailing pitifully - she had been crying for hours. It was very cold outside and she was very wet.

The mother said she did not have a name yet, she was only two months old and she did not have time to name her, there were two others at home and one on the way. My aunt asked if she had considered adoption.

Nicuta could not have children of her own and longed to raise a baby. She and her husband Nae were comfortable by Romanian standards, had a little house in the village, a small plot of land, a cow, a pig, chicken, a cat, a dog, and some money in the bank.

She was a gifted weaver, made beautiful wool rugs and tapestries. She had certainly passed the age of caring for babies, but something tugged at her heart about this yet unnamed little girl. Nicuta felt that the child deserved a better life and she was just the woman to provide a happy home. She was told no but was stubbornly undeterred.

She returned the second day to find the woman selling fruits and ignoring the crying baby while tending to her stall of apples. She was oblivious to the needs of the child. She watched her for hours. The baby was never diapered, fed, or given milk the entire time. The tiny girl was so malnourished, her face was transparently ghostly white, with blue veins running across. My aunt asked about the possibility of adoption and the mother told her no again and again.

On the third day, Nicuta returned with a police officer and a representative of the local orphanage. There were plenty orphanages under communism for unwanted and abused children, as well as for those who truly did not have any parents or were abandoned because they were imperfect.

My aunt, mom's oldest sister, wanted the baby to be taken to a proper home even though it was not going to be her house. Questions were asked and the woman was invited to the police precinct the next day.

Aunt Nicuta had to return home to Tirgsor that day. She was happy that she could help a neglected child. She left her address in case the police wanted to ask more questions.

She went home but the image of the baby was burned into her brain and could not sleep well the following nights. She told us about it, she wished she could have taken her home. She stopped talking about the incident but it remained in the back of her mind. She could not shake the feeling that she should have done more.

Two weeks later, a village police officer knocked on the door and told her that the baby she saw in Transylvania at the farmer's market was now under the custody of the state, and, if she was interested, she could apply for adoption. The mother had willingly given up the baby to the orphanage since she was overwhelmed and unable to care for her emotionally and financially. Aunt Nicuta and her husband Nae could not say "yes" fast enough.

An attorney drew up the paperwork and before the ink was even dry, uncle Nae and aunt Nicuta were back on the train on their way to Transylvania, to claim the baby from the orphanage.

They were reunited with a slightly warmer baby but still very much underweight and malnourished. She had brought beautiful embroidered little hats, clothes, and blankets that she had sewn with her own hands years ago in expectation of a pregnancy of her own. The little baby was lost in so much lace and wild eyed from all the sudden attention, cuddling and forehead kissing.

They named her Monica before they left the orphanage. She was baptized two months later when her overall health and weight had improved. My Mom offered to be the Godmother, the stand-in mother in case of unthinkable disaster. It was a beautiful celebration of life, an opportunity for family togetherness, shared love, traditions, good food, and prayer in the lovely Orthodox Church in my Grandmother's village.

A government worker was to supervise her mothering skills every day for the next six months to ensure the welfare of the child. The visits were impromptu and quite disruptive to their lives as the government intruded into every aspect of a family's life. They controlled everything from cradle to grave.

Monica grew up like a little princess, the apple of her parents' eyes. She was sent to dental school and became a prosthesis technician. She married and had two children of her own.

She never searched for her biological mother; she always said Nicuta was her mom. Her siblings, after extensive search, found her recently, but, aside from meeting them, she had no interest to pursue a familial bond. She was very devoted to her adoptive mom and dad.

Nae died a few years ago, he was partially deaf and blind but Monica and her husband took care of him until the very end. He was the gentlest man I have ever met and a great mechanic. He could probably keep any tractor running for years with improvised parts.

In the middle of summer, Nicuta, now 84 years old, with limited mobility from arthritis but otherwise healthy, was placed outside in the sun by her nurse who promised to return in 45 minutes to take her back into the house.

Four and half hours later, when the nurse finally returned, without water and shade, my loving aunt had died of sunstroke. She had tried to get her walker, which was leaning against the wall, but it was too far for her to reach. There was nobody around to ask for help; Monica and her husband were at work. She died in agony, alone.

The church bells toll for the beautiful life of Nicuta who died from socialized medicine nursing care neglect and abuse. Will the nurse be punished? No, human life has no value under socialized medicine. She was worth everything to us, her family, and especially to her loving and devoted daughter, Monica.

FIRST TRIP TO THE MALL

I like to compare the shopping trip to the mall to the Sunday Promenade in Europe. Every Sunday afternoon, we dressed up in our only good dresses and shoes, and took a bus to downtown's Republic Boulevard, flanked by beautiful old chestnut trees. At one end was the main train station terminal, at the other end, the Art Museum, the Marriage House, and a Parisian like bakery with tasty confections of chocolate that we could only afford once in a very long while. Families dressed in their Sunday best paraded their children up and down or stopped to chat or people-watch if a bench was available.

We admired or envied each other in a sad display of people watching in place of going to church. Church was "verboten" by the communists and priests barely made enough money from donations and a meager state stipend to keep the church open for baptisms, weddings, and burials.

I am not sure how many people would have gone to church instead of the weekly promenade up and down the gorgeous boulevard had God worship been allowed by the communist state.

Come to think of it, since we had state sponsored marriage houses, I think the only reason the communists kept some churches open was to bury its dead. We did not have funeral homes so the logical location to place the deceased in state was the church.

I say this because the regime had no qualms about demolishing beautiful old churches, 300-400 years old some of them, to make room for gaudy concrete buildings, headquarters of the local chapters of the communist party or the unions (syndicates as they were called). Ceausescu, the horrible dictator, had destroyed many gems of architecture to make room for his palace dedicated to megalomania and bad taste.

America's Promenade is the Mall. You can imagine my glee to be introduced to such a lovely indoor invention. Rain, snow, sunshine, oppressive heat, no problem. The mall offered comfort and the opportunity to window shop even though we had no money.

I was surprised that shoppers could actually try things on in a very cozy dressing room, helped by polite ladies and, most shocking of all, could actually return things if they changed their minds.

I was used to the communist central planning that would produce half a million white boots when the market demanded 10 million pairs of black and brown boots. People would fight in long lines for the white boots anyway, sometimes grabbing the first pair on the rack, not knowing whether that was the right size or not. Not that it mattered, you were not allowed to try them on, you might get them dirty. Neither were you allowed to return them if they did not fit. Once you bought them, they were yours to keep. No returns, no exchanges, no credit. I can only imagine that there were many customers with sore feet and bunions. Romanian shoes were not exactly made for comfort or durability.

People only bathed once a week and I could understand why the rule was imposed that clothes could not be tried on. It is not that people did not wish to bathe, water was scarce, soap expensive and hard to find, shampoo unheard of, and deodorant pricey and hard to procure.

Cultural differences made shopping at the mall awkward and sometimes uncomfortable situations ensued.

I apologized to a poor girl who was politely trying to sell spoon rings, silver rings wrapped around the finger made from the end of a spoon. Coming from such a poor country, it seemed excessive to me to destroy a perfectly good spoon in order to create such a gaudy ring.

I wasted no time telling the girl the truth; after all, Europeans are very blunt, not necessarily schooled in the fine American art of tactfulness. I never fully understood the art of deception wrapped into a sweet, fake smile. A very sharp dagger in the back was sure to follow.

I will certainly never be an American politician and will never understand why a person has to apologize for expressing opinion and telling the truth. The PC police has gone too far.

I found it bizarre that people excused themselves ad nauseam if they came within the three feet of comfort zone of a passerby. Europeans get in each other's face when they talk and nobody says, "Excuse me," if they come too close to a stranger.

Speaking of being truthful and blunt, you never ask an European how they feel, unless you are prepared to listen exactly to what ails them, why, and what they are going to do about it.

I was shocked when people were using checks and credit cards. For the longest time, I could not understand the concept of personal checks, credit cards, and the responsibility that came with them. As long as I had checks, I could continue shopping, I thought.

Back in 1978, department stores did not have an instant connection with a bank clearinghouse for checks or credit cards. They were mostly accepted on faith and in some instances, by making lengthy phone calls.

My Egyptian friend, Lula, used to laugh that the country was run on paper and plastic, not fiat money. She had no idea how true her jocular statement was.

I loved the colorful department store bags and was amazed that they were given free of charge with each purchase. I saved them for a while, hoping to find other uses for them. I did the same with Styrofoam containers, plastic forks and spoons, I could not throw them away - I washed them repeatedly until they broke. My husband chided me that I was McDonald's bag lady.

I found the mall to be very peaceful, a place to meet friends, a place to relax, not necessarily to shop. There were no food courts or restaurants inside the mall . If you wanted coffee, you had to percolate it yourself – no Starbucks nearby.

The biggest department stores inside the mall in Tupelo, MS were Sears and Roebuck and J. C. Penney. There was a small McRae's. A powerful tornado destroyed part of the mall the following year; many businesses closed or moved. Tupelo was such a tornado alley. Years later, a much larger mall was built at Barnes Crossing.

A house similar to Grandma Elizabeta's (www.mycountry.ro)

POVERTY

Poverty is faith in government who is robbing the population blind while leading it over a cliff. Poverty is ignorance and illiteracy. Poverty is accepting your fate of servitude without as much as a whimper. Poverty is misplacing your trust in ordinary men while neglecting God. Poverty is a lack of hygiene. Poverty is watching your children and loved ones die because you failed to wash your hands or obtain clean water.

Poverty is watching 3 million people die of malaria worldwide in the misplaced belief that DDT is worse. Poverty is death by famine near silos full of genetic engineered corn and grain. Poverty is being unable to get clean water.

Poverty is accepting welfare and expecting entitlements from an omniscient and omnipotent government. Poverty is losing the will to fight to better your station in life. Westerners understand poverty as the difference between haves and haves not.

I remember the conversation I have had with my former mother-in-law long time ago. We were talking about Romanian poverty and I said that I was poor. Jane believed my statement to be false.

I considered myself poor since I did not have a dime to my name, a home, or any wealth. I was 21 years old, freshly off the communist boat so to speak.

Jane's explanation was that I could not possibly be poor, I was married to her son, we lived in their nicely appointed ranch home, her son ran the farm, and they had money in the bank.

Many Americans would respond to the question, are you poor, with a resonant yes. The reason most people answer yes is that they confuse wealth and income. They are short of cash in their pockets, others have no money in the bank, some do not own the car or home of their dreams, or have no accumulated wealth. They may be cash poor but are even poorer in certain commodities for which they are willing to give up their cash.

Some Americans feel entitled to the wealth of others, to free medical care, free housing, free education, free childcare, free cars, free homes, and free vacations. These same Americans welcome social engineering and promote social justice. They are willing to give up their freedoms in exchange for total government care and control of their every need.

Are we really poor in America? By most standards, Americans are not poor. Even homeless people have more wealth when compared to many citizens of other countries. Poverty is thus relative to most people. Poverty does not make one sad just as wealth does not make one happy. Some people do not even realize how poor they are, they are blissfully ignorant of reality, or may not even understand that such a concept of poverty exists. There are very poor people on this earth who are truly happy and very rich people who are miserable unless they are constantly making money or stealing other people's money in the name of wealth redistribution.

Years ago, Americans with a liberal agenda took a group of homegrown homeless to Russia to demonstrate the evils of capitalism that allowed these people to be homeless. They wanted to contrast by example the generosity of communism to its people in the face of homelessness.

The Russians stormed out of the building in disgust when they found out that these so-called "homeless" did not work. How did they expect sympathy from the Russians when they made no effort to work? The soviets' philosophy was simple, if you did not work, do not complain that you are homeless.

A bogus study has determined the income of $75,000 to be the magical number that makes people strive to achieve in order to be happy. Once this magical number is reached, there is no point in trying for more because you are not going to find happiness. This is a blatant attempt by liberal academics to justify a sad mismanagement of the economy by the ruling elites, an economy lacking jobs paying $75,000 or more per year.

There is no point in trying to be rich like us, the bogus study implied, we are so miserable making so much money, it is better to be poor and to wait on government unemployment checks or welfare.

People living under communism did not live pampered lives and the communist government did very little to improve their lot in life, just a bare minimum. The Utopian society in which everyone was equal was not so egalitarian after all.

Everyone lived in ugly and drab concrete apartments, sparsely furnished, and paid similar rents. The government decided what the needs of each family were and that was how far anyone could advance, if you can call that progress.

Few families actually owned their own home in the city. Anemic bulbs provided intermittent lighting when the party did not shut the power off for reasons of conservation or inability to produce or pay for enough electricity.

The ruling elite occupied elegant villas that had been forcefully confiscated from businesses and individuals after the rightful owners were jailed on trumped up "crimes against the communist ideology."

The elaborate grey apartment complexes in the city had five to nine stories with semi-finished stairwells. Nine story buildings had elevators that constantly trapped its riders for hours when power outages occurred or from lack of proper maintenance. The common area and the stairwells were the responsibility of each renter to maintain and clean. Fines were levied if people did not take turns to clean the stairs. The garbage bay was always nasty, smelly, and unsanitary since the city provided these services whenever they saw fit.

Kids played in very large groups and nobody supervised them to make sure they were safe. They were often run over by cars while playing in the streets, on the sidewalks, or crossing the road. People used sidewalks for parking, with total disregard for the law, which was never enforced.

Very few people owned a TV or radios and phones were even scarcer. One in ten apartments owned a TV and it was customary to invite the whole street over in the home with a TV if a good movie, football game, or concert was playing. That was not a frequent occurrence since the communists only broadcast two stations in black and white, both heavy on constant propaganda and nauseating 24/7 speeches by the communist dictator.

Radios were more common but people had to pay a fiscal monthly tax for the right to own both a radio and a TV, a type of subscription that one had to pay whether they had an antenna or not. Inspectors came into homes unannounced to check ownership of TVs and radios, and compliance with the fiscal tax.

Phones were rarer because it took close to 14 years to have a phone installed from the time application was made until it was actually installed. My parents applied for a phone when I was in kindergarten and we did not get it until I was in 12th grade! There was a joke about a person going to the post office to fill out a request for phone installation and the clerk told the customer that it would be in 14 years. The customer asked whether it will be a.m. or p.m. Irritated, the clerk answered, "what difference does it make, it is 14 years from now." The customer answered calmly, "The plumber is coming in the morning."

Because everyone earned the same amount of money, there was no incentive to excel, to work harder, or to go the extra mile. The work ethic was, "we pretend to work, and they pretend to pay us." My Dad, who was a mechanic, was responsible for several men in his crew at the refinery. Most days his charges were hard to find because they were hiding in different areas or trenches, asleep. The work ethic was non-existent thanks to the low pay and the communist mentality to give everybody a living wage for just showing up, not based on performance. Lack of incentives to work harder made everybody lazier and less responsible for their workplace. Lackadaisical employees caused more accidents and unnecessary deaths.

Country folk were a little better off - they could grow a garden and raise farm animals, a luxury that city people did not have. They could also own a modest home, some better than others. In some far away villages, homes were made of bricks built of mud mixed with straw. It was cheap and a great insulator both in winter and summertime - and a great burrowing and hiding place for mice and rats. Some homes were built of wood, brick, and stucco but lacked basic amenities such as electricity, indoor plumbing, and running water.

A small barn provided winter shelter for farm animals. Dogs were kept outside in a doghouse, poor creatures, but cats had better lives indoors. Dogs were more utilitarian than pets in the sense of providing guard to the owner or the flock of sheep. Only large animals were tended to by vets. It was a luxury - real vets were hard to find. A person with some vet training sufficed.

Even in times of food shortages, village people had chickens, cows, pigs, and gardens to feed their families. A small plot could raise enough corn and vegetables to sustain them through winter. It was harder getting rice, flour, and oil and other basic staples. The communist co-operative who had forced everybody to give up their lands for the "common good" would force villagers to work in the fields, back breaking work, for a small percentage of the crop in the fall.

The government took the lion's share, what was left was divided among the collective villagers who had plowed, seeded, weeded, hoed, and harvested the wheat, corn, or whatever crop the collective cooperative had planted on directions from the communist party planners.

The common land and collective labor concept did not work very well since some villagers were more industrious and motivated than others yet the remainder of the crops was equally shared. This angered those who worked harder to see the fruits of their labor go to lazy villagers who did not contribute much work to the crops.

The crop and industry planners had no experience in any of the sectors they made life and death decision on and often no formal education, but they were considered the "experts." Their only qualification was membership in the communist party and the ability to change their views on command as the wind blew from the direction of the dictator president and his wife who was very much involved in politics and economic planning.

Children had few toys and improvised creatively for entertainment and play. I personally owned one doll, a doll bed, a teddy bear, and a set of 9-block puzzle that could assemble a different picture on each side of the cube. I felt extremely lucky when my grandfather cobbled together a sled from a few wooden slats and two pieces of heavy iron, which he welded together. This sled gave me endless hours of joy and many scrapes and bruises.

My grandfather was the kind of man who could make MacGyver proud - he put together repair parts for the villager's bikes and motorcycles. He never charged them; he bartered or expected nothing in return. I watched him in fascination when he welded bike tires with glue and pliers. I used to joke that grandpa could fix anything with dirt and spit.

Everybody owned one nice outfit and pair of shoes, which they only wore on special holidays: Easter, Christmas, baptisms, weddings, or funerals. The rest of the year, villagers went about happily in their bare feet and some old, sun washed, well-worn outfit. City folk at least wore shoes all the time. They had to; there was too much debris and opportunities to get hurt. Every summer I got a new pair of sandals and every winter a new pair of boots. They were usually ill fitting and caused me years of pain and surgery later in life.

The sparsely, Spartan furnished apartments had a bed and a wardrobe; there were no such things as walk-in closets. Our kitchen, hallway, and bathroom were about the size of a large walk-in closet. I think our entire apartment was the size of our master bedroom, bath, and walk-in closet. We had a living room that doubled as dining room and my bedroom. It contained a bed, a couch, a dining table with three chairs and a bookcase.

The one bedroom, my parents', had a bed, a black and white TV, and a wardrobe. That is how rich we were because the communist party had decided those to be our only needs based on the pay my parents received in exchange for their hard labor, as in the communist mantra, "to each according to their needs."

The kitchen had a small cupboard, a sink, and a table with two chairs. We took turns to eat since we could not sit together for dinner, we did not have enough chairs or space. When I was in high school, my parents had bought a very small, dorm-sized refrigerator that we placed in the hallway because there was no room in the kitchen.

Few people owned a car and most of us took the bus anywhere or walked. Children were not ferried to school by buses; nobody was fed breakfasts or lunch at school. We were lucky if we had something home to eat.

Nobody went on vacations and travel abroad was impossible since the government only gave visas to very special people who were part of the communist milieu.

Citizens had very little contact with the outside world, save for listening to Voice of America or Free Europe via short wave radio. Such broadcasts kept our hopes alive for a better life. We had to be very careful and turn the volume down since the thin walls had ears. We generally knew who the government snitches were in the apartment complex, but we were never sure if a new informant had been hired. We had a good underground system of notifying each other even though there was no Internet.

Hollywood gave us a fantasized world of America and glimpses of celluloid life in everyday America, or at least, what we thought everyday America to be. Many of us really thought money grew on trees for Americans. They were not blessed because they worked hard, were entrepreneurs, and free, but because they were born rich, or stole from the producers. The communist propaganda encouraged this false view.

The first few years after moving to the U.S., every friend and relative sent letters requesting blue jeans, food, and medicine, thinking that they cost a pittance in such a rich country. It did not matter that I was poor as a church mouse and could not afford my own medicine, clothes, or visits to the doctor. How could I be poor in America, the land of opportunity, they said? My family could not understand that wealth took time and hard work to create and income would come later with the opportunity to better myself.

Cities had museums, theater, and cinema, and although not very expensive by western standards, few Romanians could afford to go since there were other needs that had to be met before a movie, a play, or a visit to the museum.

Larger villages, closer to a metropolis had movie showings once a month in the collective co-op meeting center. John Wayne was everybody's popular hero and his movies played repeatedly, with subtitles. In fact, I taught myself English by watching John Wayne movies. I could hear the American English and repeat and mimic his accent. This resulted often in mispronunciation since proper diction was not the goal of a movie dialog. I later took two years of English in high school and learned proper British English.

Medical care was free to all, but the quality and availability of it was very poor. Villagers were worse off since their care was relegated to a nurse with 6 months of training and the ambulance took days to arrive with no help, medicine, or life saving support, just a driver. Each village had a co-op store with a few supplies of necessities, none of which included food.

Villagers had to take the bus into town if they needed staples such as flour, sugar, cooking oil, and rice. The bus made twice a day runs, if it was closer, 10 miles or less, to a metropolis. If the village was remote, there were no bus routes and the villagers traveled by wagons once every so many months to get supplies for several families. They were totally cut off from civilization although they may have been only 35 miles from a large town.

And yet we were so much better off than other third world countries. That is to say, poverty is relative; there is always someone who is worse off than you are. Many have asked, if I had to choose, where would I live? Taking into account the opportunities I have had to succeed, the freedom, and the standard of living, United States is still the best country in the world to be poor in.

Ileana in a strange Santa sleigh

Ileana with parents in a bizarre Santa scene

Wearing one of grandma's scratchy but warm sweaters

CHRISTMAS

All communist holidays were secularized, including Christmas. There was not even a hint of pretense that anything about the communist society was Christian or based on a very strong Judeo-Christian tradition. The only concession to Christianity that Mom was allowed to make without going to jail was to have our parish priest come to our home and bless it every Christmas and Easter.

He was a very handsome man with deep blue eyes who spoke so many foreign languages that he inspired me to try to be like him. I owe some of my linguistic ability to a very erudite person who could read Latin and Greek with ease.

People did not get the day off at Christmas but celebrated the New Year's Day, a secular, communist sanctioned holiday. Christmas was not about gift giving, it was about togetherness with friends and family, cheer, and good food. It was a one time a year opportunity to eat well. The communist party supplied the stores with more food, the lines were shorter, there was more booze delivered to grocery stores, and an anemic Christmas tree was decorated with lights in some of the larger cities.

Some families bought their own blue spruce or pine and decorated it with real candles, apples, cookies, and homemade paper ornaments. I remember owning a few real ornaments, given to me by my grandparents. Ornaments were available but very expensive. Candles were lit with care a few minutes at night to avoid fires. It was such a delightful treat to find a few oranges and cookies hanging on colorful strings and home-made paper baskets decorated with crepe paper and filled with candy, chocolate, or raisins.

The larger towns had a winter carnival with rides during the second half of December. The city tried to decorate a large fir tree with colored lights. A thin Santa Clause (Mos Craciun) made his appearance, taking photographs with children outdoors on a sleigh.

St. Nicholas was someone to be feared. Everybody knew the true story and tried very hard to behave all year long. Children left their shoes outside the door on December 6. If they were good, St. Nicholas left candy, fragrant oranges, bananas, and chocolates. If kids misbehaved, they found a lump of coal or a switch in their shoes.

On Christmas Eve poor parents would leave a small toy under the pillow. Children of ruling elites were luckier, attended lavish Christmas parties and received many gifts.

Some Romanians did not go to church on Christmas Eve to pray as many churches were closed. Villagers were more fortunate because priests opened the modest churches for liturgy during the holidays. I have attended services many times on Christmas Eve with my Aunt Leana. She was cantor and deacon. I loved her Gregorian Chants. Church was more active so far away from the prying eyes of communists.

The village was perched on this remote mountain of salt and because it was so inaccessible, the communists tended to leave it alone. People had small, productive orchards and vineyards because it was not feasible for the communists to take over their land as it was so spread out on top of the mountain.

Caroling and donations of food to very poor families with widowed parents were the highlight of Christmas. We went from house to house with elaborately prepared plates of food and baskets of goodies. We used large horse drawn sleighs or wagons to deliver the food. Both adults and children caroled outside the front door.

One tradition observed in most parts of the country, Wallachia, Moldova, and Transylvania was the slaughter of a pig at Christmas. I always refused to watch the slaughter of my Grandfather's pig the week before Christmas. I could hear the squeals of pain and saw the blood in the white snow. It always made me squeamish and sad.

The pig provided sustenance for the entire extended family for months to come. The meat was smoked into ham, deep-fried and preserved in large lard vats, and made into sausages smoked in the attic. Salt was a natural preservative and needless to say many adults had issues with high blood pressure from salt and lard. Some of the meat was cooked fresh on open pits outdoors and the family gathered around the fire to celebrate the abundance of food and the flowing wine. Even small children were handed glasses of ruby red wine, most of it produced on the premises or in the village. I ate many hearty meals cooked on a cast iron top, wood burning stove that channeled hot air to other rooms in the house via primitive mud brick ducts.

Villagers bartered things they had in excess with other neighbors since money was so tight. Services were also bartered, one learned to adjust to being poor in so many creative ways. My Grandmother and her middle daughter learned to be tailors and made dresses. Her youngest daughter was a skilled accountant. Her oldest daughter was a master weaver - she made beautiful fabrics and wool rugs. My own Grandmother knew how to spin the coat of a sheep into beautiful yarn, dyed it herself with vegetable dyes, and knew how to knit warm and scratchy sweaters.

I grew up in Grandma's sweaters since my parents could not afford to buy expensive clothes. And they were all expensive when we lived on such meager incomes. My godmother made my dresses. She could take key measurements of my body, and with chalk, make an outline of the various dress pieces on fabric without a pattern, cut them with scissors, and voila, a new, not so trendy dress would emerge. She stitched it together on Grandma's 80-year-old Singer pedal activated sewing machine. We did not care about fashion, we were glad to have something to keep us covered and warm.

Grown men would go caroling in the village on January 1 to herald the arrival of the New Year. Dressed in traditional costumes, they walked beside a sled pulled by horses. A young green fir decorated with colorful paper ornaments was perched on the sled. Singing and cracking their whips, they demanded pay in food or money from each home. People gave small tokens of their poverty because they believed in sharing as a virtue.

Larger cities had an area reserved for rides for small children and it was the highlight of my year because sometimes the scary Saint Nicholas made his appearance. Children could actually take their black and white pictures with "Santa."

My parents were my secret Mos Craciun on the eve of December 24, they always put a small food item under my pillow - a chocolate bar, a bag of candy, a perfect apple, an exquisite orange from Jerusalem wrapped in fine tissue paper, or a perfect banana from Greece, with their exotic aromas of forbidden and out of reach fruit for mere mortals. I would imagine what would be like to pluck the fruit from its faraway Mediterranean location and to bask in the glorious sun as snow and ice were blanketing our surroundings.

Christmas was abundant with snow and gave us kids the opportunity to sled downhill and to have our fathers drag us up and down the street in home-made sleds. It was sheer happiness. Our moms would layer our clothes so much, we could hardly move. The key ingredient to staying warm was the flannel pajamas underneath all the clothes. We played in the snow from the time we woke up until nightfall. We forgot about hunger and thirst. We did not want to miss one minute of fun in the snow. By the time we returned home, our clothes were so wet from sledding, ice skating, falling and getting up, that they froze stiff on our bodies. Nobody had hypothermia or lost any limbs to frostbite. We were happy and oblivious to our state in life.

MY FIRST BAPTIST CHURCH VISIT

Sam and I attended Mantee Baptist Church where his parents were members. I was surprised by the best Sunday dress attire and the country club atmosphere. I was running through my mind the content of my meager wardrobe and I did not seem to find any matches for a suitable Sunday service dress. Any event that required dressing up meant that I would have to borrow a dress, as I had no money for frivolous purchases.

I certainly have never seen cookies, coffee, and socializing in our crumbling churches. Orthodox churches had a mystical aura, with their old icons, paintings, candles, incense, statues, and other religious symbols. I felt the presence of God and feared retribution oozing from the medieval walls adorned with symbols of past reverence. I feared that God's wrath might strike sinners for past transgressions. There were no stools or comfortable chairs for parishioners, we had to kneel on cold concrete or at best carry a pillow from home. The ornate chairs lining the walls were reserved for the deacons and the very elderly patrons of the church, the regulars. During almost 30 years of communist reign, very few people dared to show up in church regularly for fear of retribution. The elderly had very little to lose and the regime left them alone. We went to church on Easter, Christmas, for baptisms, weddings, and burials. If you wanted to keep your job, you had to stay away from church. Bibles were hard to find, they were bought, sold, read, and studied underground. Hymnals were impossible to procure as they were passed from generation to generation, from one cantor to another.

The very poor and destitute congregated around the existing churches, supported by the elderly parishioners' donations and the food donated by families who celebrated weddings, baptisms, and burials. It was customary to cook and give certain foods to the poor "in memoriam" of the deceased, the newlyweds, and the newly baptized.

The American Bible Society had donated thousands of beautiful Bibles but Nicolae Ceausescu, the communist dictator, had ordered them recycled into toilet paper. The print was so exquisite, and their recycling so poor, that Bible verses were still visible on the toilet paper. It was blasphemy and I refused to use it. I used newspapers. I preferred ink on my behind, I did not want to deface the word of God.

Toilet paper was a precious commodity at that time. Many rolls were so poorly made that I could see wood splinters through the paper. I saved a small roll years later for show and tell for my students and, to this day, they do not believe it. The toilet paper was brownish in color. Americans are so spoiled by Charmin and its abundance, they have no idea how other people live and that life can be any other way but good.

We spent an hour in church during which time we sang, prayed, and listened to the sonorous voice of the preacher. To this day, I have a hard time remembering sermons - after the first two or three sentences my mind wonders off. It is not that I am disrespectful or uninterested; I daydream when the cadence of the preacher's voice is monotonous. My mind wanders in marvelous places.

Orthodox priests wear different garments and ceremonial attire that is significant to their position. Somehow, I could not associate a suit-wearing person with a priest. I was not questioning their religiosity at all; it was just harder to listen, the mysticism was dispelled by the suit, it was too mundane. I would stare at the bare walls in our Baptist church and I would miss the beautiful icons, the crucifixes, and other religious symbols from the orthodox faith.

The liturgy lasted so much longer in the orthodox religion, I was pleasantly surprised at the shortness of the Baptist service, by comparison. Sunday school was a novelty too, lay people were not supposed to teach religion. So I thought.

In the end, running through the gauntlet of parishioners, Sam introduced me to everybody, nice, kind, God fearing people who gawked at me, pinched me, talked about me as if I was not even there, was deaf or dumb, or as if I was not a legal alien, but a bona fide alien from Mars. Nobody had heard of Romania, it might as well have been a crater on Mars.

People took an interest in me, some felt sorry for me because my parents were so far away. Others chose to ignore me because I was an intruder and did not belong. A few parishioners decided to make me their charity project as I had no clothes, no job, and my southern language skills were quite limited. One woman whom I remember with fondness, Gail, bought my very first pair of blue jeans. I was elated; I still remember the trip we took to the local department store in Houston.

Rural Mississippians did not travel much outside of their communities, much less outside of their state in the 70s. They are salt of the earth kind of people and generous to a fault. As I found out much later, Governor Finch told me, I was the only Romanian in the great State of Mississippi in 1979. He was looking for a translator for the International Ballet Competition in Jackson and found me. It was a lonely and disheartening feeling to know that I was the only one of a particular ethnic group. Talk about being a minority of one!

Orthodox Church at Tusnad

RELIGION

Most people do not understand what orthodox is - they think Jewish. I am not sure most orthodox people truly understand the mystical side of their religion. I can feel it when I enter a majestic cathedral in Europe, richly decorated with lavish columns, statues, icons, and symbols lost in translation and in our understanding.

I was torn many times, upon standing inside St. Peter's Basilica, between my feelings of awe at the magnificent and opulent construction and my feelings of sorrow at the sacrifice so many millions of poor people had to make in order that such a jewel of architecture and art could be enjoyed by generations after generations. Did they starve in order to pay heavy taxes, what horrid living conditions had they endured, were they forced to work long hours for meager pay in order that this basilica be built?

Orthodox religion predates Catholicism by a year or two. If you ask a catholic, they will tell you Catholicism is the oldest organized form of religion in existence. Some historians and orthodox themselves believe The Orthodox Church to be the One, established 2,000 years ago by Jesus Christ and his Apostles.

Daddy used to tell me that our family originated with the Apostles since our last name is Apostolescu, Romanian for "of the Apostles." I am sure that was not true, but it made interesting conversation.

Christianity struggled to exist during Roman times when they were forced to worship in tunnels underground Rome. Domitila's catacombs contain one of the first underground Christian churches. I was a bit uneasy when I visited the catacombs. It had not crossed my mind how close we were to Mount Vesuvius until the tour guide mentioned it. I tried not to panic. On my second visit, this time with my husband David, he had to coax me into going underground again. It was a truly mystical experience, tranquil, and frightening at the same time.

The Orthodox Church is officially called the Orthodox Catholic Church and commonly referred to as the Eastern Orthodox Church. The Church is composed of several self-governing ecclesial bodies, each geographically and nationally distinct.

Each self-governing branch, often representing a nation, is led by a synod of bishops whose duty, among other things, is to preserve and teach the Apostolic traditions and church practices. As in the Roman Catholic Church, Anglican Church, Oriental Orthodoxy and some other churches, Orthodox bishops trace their lineage back to the Apostles through the process of Apostolic Succession.

The Orthodox Church claims to trace its development back through the Byzantine or Roman Empire, to the earliest church established by St. Paul and the Apostles.

After baptism, a person receives the Holy Spirit and must begin a spiritual pilgrimage of being more holy and "Christ Like." Most babies are baptized shortly after birth and there is a Godmother holding the newborn at the altar while the ceremony is performed. She is a stand-in mom in case something happens to the real mom.

The Godmother is revered, loved, respected, and celebrated through her entire life. There are special occasions when parties are given in her honor, celebrations of life, family, togetherness, and familial alliance.

My Godmother was Aunt Stela, who passed away a year ago. Although I miss her terribly, I feel blessed that I was able to speak to her weekly until the last few days of her life when she was in and out of consciousness.

The Biblical text used by the Orthodox includes the Greek Septuagint and the New Testament. It includes the seven Deuterocanonical Books which are generally rejected by Protestants and a small number of other books that are in neither Western canon. These books are used in the Divine Liturgy.

Icons adorn the walls of Eastern Orthodox churches and cover the inside structure completely. There is an interior mat around the painted face of a Saint, Mary, or Baby Jesus. The mat is hammered out of solid silver. Jesus Christ is depicted during the crucifixion, in a life size statue. Worshippers kiss the statue's feet during prayer.

Countryside Orthodox homes have an area set aside for family prayer, an altar, usually an eastern facing wall, on which simple icons and prayer beads hang. Orthodox believers cross themselves during prayer opposite from Catholics.

The calculation of Orthodox Easter is very complex, the Sunday following Paschal full moon, pronounced, "Pas-kul." Easter Sunday is the date of the annual celebration of Christ's resurrection.

The Easter Dating Method has to maintain the same season of the year and the same relationship to the preceding astronomical full moon that occurred at the time of his resurrection in 30 A.D. Easter dates vary and very seldom coincide with the Protestant Easter.

There was the jocular story of the priest who kept kernels of corn in his jacket to be able to tell parishioners how many days were left until Easter. He would quickly count how many kernels of corn he had left in his jacket pocket after he had carefully thrown one kernel out each day. His housekeeper had thought, upon discovering his stash of corn, that the Father liked corn, so she added a handful into his pocket. When he met with a parishioner and was asked how many days until Easter, he proceeded to count the corn. Exasperated, after he counted and counted, with no end in sight, he told the parishioner that there was not going to be Easter that year after all.

Certainly, there was no Orthodox Sunday School to attend and nobody taught us lessons from the Bible. Older females in the family would tell stories each evening after supper, while we sat around on benches outside in the garden or by the side of the road.

All homes were surrounded by tall wood fences and had a very large bench in front of the main gate, outside the fence. This bench was the gathering place for many villagers who happened to walk by on their way home. I heard many fascinating Biblical stories this way, sitting at my grandparents' feet. Most stories were true accounts of the Bible; others were embellished by the storyteller to entice the young minds to search for themselves.

Aunt Leana, who was a cantor and deacon at Popesti Orthodox Church, had a well-worn Bible from which she would read stories every time I visited. She had an oil lamp by her side, large magnifying glasses tied with a string, and a large bowl of fresh fruit and grapes from her orchard. We sat on the porch or in her tiny and cozy two-room mud brick house. When her eyes got tired, she would start singing Gregorian chants and nasalized humming which she often did, accompanying the readings during Liturgy.

We had no Bible lessons - 40 years or more of communist rule forbade the owning of a Bible, open prayer, Bible study in school, and church attendance. Believers were ridiculed as missing their marbles. Atheism was the state religion. The only people who were semi-free to observe their religion were the elderly. The communists decided that they already had a foot in the grave and one on the proverbial banana peel, who cared if they went to church? Consequently, most of the regulars were little old ladies. That is because men died much sooner than women - men pretty much counted on being survived by their wives. These women helped the priest with daily chores, cleaned the church, polished the silver icons, mended the kneeling pillows, cleaned the candle wax off the floors and candle holders, tended the surrounding gardens, planted the flowers, the shrubs, and cut the grass around cemetery plots with a scythe.

Easter and Christmas were the only holidays when church attendance grew tenfold. The commie handlers allowed the masses to celebrate, but took notes cautiously and carefully. We carried lit candles at midnight around the church, sang Gregorian chants, prayed and celebrated our humanity from God. Food was brought to church and shared with everybody in remembrance of Christ and beloved family members who passed away.

There were Catholics in Transylvania in western Romania, among Swabians and Hungarians, a few Baptists here and there, Lutherans in western Transylvania, and Muslims in eastern Romania, at the Black Sea, close to the European side of Istanbul. I remember visiting a mosque with my aunt at the Black Sea - it was more like a museum visit, the mosque was empty. Neither faith enjoyed much freedom; they were on par with the Orthodox. The only concession made was the use of language, i.e., German, Hungarian, and Arabic.

The American Bible Society had donated Bibles to the state after a terrible earthquake - they wanted the victims to find comfort in the word of God. The state, however, decided to recycle them into toilet paper. The quality of print and material was so good and the quality of manufacture so poor that the words of the Bible were still legible on the rolls of toilet paper. I had just started studying English and I pointed that out to my Dad. We were appalled and saddened by the offensive abuse of the Holy Book.

Baptisms, funerals, and weddings were certainly not frowned upon. Communist elites tried to replace weddings with civil ceremonies, but most people preferred to have both. The church ceremony was always viewed as more meaningful. Everybody had to be baptized and given a name, even commies accepted that. And, of course, funerals, nobody escaped death, and, since there were no funeral homes, churches were the logical place for the last rites and passage to the other world. The last ride to the cemetery was done with pomp and circumstance, a funeral band, and a horse-drawn carriage or a large truck bed, depending on the status of the deceased.

SUPERSTITIONS

Because my ancestors were both Romans and Dacians, I have superstition DNA running through my blood. I did not realize the degree of infection until I had my first child. Every day I changed Mimi's crib sheets I would find a large butcher knife under her mattress. I would take it and put it back in the kitchen. The next day, the knife would re-appear. It was so odd, it did not occur to me to ask mom why the knife was there every day. Then one day, without explanation, the knife disappeared. When I finally did ask mom, she explained that knives protected babies from evil spirits until they were baptized. Sure enough, Mimi had been baptized the day before.

This reminded me of the fairy tale in which the king invited the fairies to cast good spells on his newborn but forgot to invite the thin-skinned one. The uninvited fairy gifted the little girl with a life of misery, locked in a castle until Prince Charming would appear to rescue her from a seemingly impossible-to-climb tower.

I knew about the proverbial black cat crossing the road. I always returned home when that happened, no matter where I was going, including school. I knew a bad grade or occurrence were sure to follow. To cure such bad luck, Romanians spit nine times and said an incantation before avoiding the black cat.

Mom and Grandma Elena thought that wearing a shirt inside out meant that one was cheating on his/her spouse. My response was always, mom, I don't have a spouse, and what is a spouse? Was this somehow related to the English phrase, "turncoat?"

The salt over the left shoulder was definitely Roman - it cast away evil spirits lurking around the dinner table. Walking under a ladder was also a bad idea. A broken mirror brought seven years of bad luck.

Sneezing was a dangerous time since it was believed that, for a brief moment, the soul left the body and evil spirits could crawl in. People nearby would wish "noroc," "good luck," to keep the evil spirits from inhabiting your body while the soul was floating somewhere in the air.

Crossing yourself three times prevented bad luck and possible misfortune when embarking on a new journey, new school, new job, or adventure.

Families in mourning had to wear black for six months or the deceased could not rest in peace. Close family members could not shave, wash their hair, comb their hair, look in a mirror or the deceased would become a ghost.

If it rained on the day of the funeral or during the funeral, it was a sign that the deceased was sorry to go and had regrets that she/he had not expressed before their final breath.

Babies that had not been baptized and passed away could not be buried in the regular cemetery; they had plots outside the fence, as their bodies might be corrupted by evil spirits lurking in a holy place.

Newborns wore red ribbons tied or sewn into their little hats to protect them from the evil eye. Romans and Romanians truly believed that, if you had blue or green eyes, you had the power to bewitch a person and change their state of health and well-being. To escape a terrible fate from the evil eye, a special incantation had to be said over a glass of fresh water from a spring into which a burning match was extinguished. The recipient of the evil eye had to drink the water in order to destroy the potential effect of any evil spell.

Brides had to step into their home with their right foot first. To do so with the left foot was sinister and invited terrible misfortune in the marriage. "Sinistra" was Latin for left, hence the English word, sinister. To prevent brides from tripping, a sign of bad luck, the groom would carry them over the threshold. The posts of the house were oiled for good luck.

During the church wedding ceremony, two very large white candles, the height of a person and about five inches in diameter, decorated with a fresh flower bouquet, were lit and held by a bridesmaid and the groom's best man. The first candle to flicker out represented the death of that person.

Upon eyeing someone with a particular condition or witnessing a scary situation, the viewer would spit sideways three times and cross themselves three times to avoid a similar fate. This included seeing a black cat in the vicinity.

Knocking on wood three times as in the Holy Trinity was a way to ward off evil spirits who might lurk nearby, or avoid the possibility of similar injury, i.e., knock on wood.

Children were not supposed to talk or sing at the dinner table or else risk marrying a gypsy. Since nobody wanted to live in a tent and travel in a covered wagon, kids were pretty quiet at suppertime. I may have told mom at least a couple of times that I did not care since gypsies made good roasted sunflowers and I wanted to be a sunflower vendor when I grew up. My defiance exasperated my Mother who always feared that the gypsy vendors would kidnap her only child. The fear was not misplaced since gypsies kidnapped children regularly to indoctrinate them into stealing, thus providing a steady income for the caravan.

Whenever I had a headache, Mom was convinced that I was a victim of the evil eye. She would make me sit still, moved around me three times while she mumbled incantations, and then my headache was supposed to disappear. Too bad the nerve endings on my scalp were not getting the memo. This pseudo-method was never demonstrated that it worked, but Mom and many others like her tried it and believed in it anyway.

A person with blue or green eyes had the power to cast a spell of evil on someone they disliked by staring at them intently and crossing themselves three times. If the receiver of the evil eye became aware of the intent, he/she would spit three times to avoid the bad fate.

Fear of ghosts was very powerful. Families followed strict funeral customs to prevent the deceased from returning and exacting retribution. Some villagers built homes with a special door through which the coffin exited the home. This door was forever sealed and never re-opened.

How can both educated and uneducated people believe in superstitions? Ignorance and fear of the unknown can plague anybody, including atheists and agnostics.

CULTURAL DIFFERENCES

As an 18 year old in Romania, it has never occurred to me that cultural differences can doom a marriage. As a typical naive teenager, I truly believed that people were the same, no matter what country they came from. We laughed, cried, experienced emotion, hurt, love, and enjoyed the simple pleasures in life the same way. What can cultural differences possibly do to one's relationship with another human being of the opposite sex? Quite a lot, I found out along the way.

For starters, growing up with freedom and taking it for granted, made enduring the indignities of living under a dictatorship quite unbearable. As an American, one can enter pretty much any official or government building. Not so under communism.

I was shocked the first time I was allowed to enter a U.S. air force base and move about without ever being asked who I was or what I was doing there. We had clearance and business to enter. In Romania we were not even allowed within miles and miles of a military base, a sort of area 51, no man's land. If you dared approach the forbidden area, you did so at your own risk, you would be shot.

Government buildings were off limits to its citizens, but particularly to foreigners. My husband Sam could not understand why he was not allowed to enter government buildings or communist party centers.

His frustration grew and grew with every new rule and regulation he encountered that stifled his freedom to move about, to be who he was, a free man. He took out his frustration on the nearest person who was always beside him, me.

When our oldest daughter was four years old, she unwittingly jumped into a water fountain located in front of the communist party headquarters. Unknown to us, underneath the fountain was a specialized shopping center for the ruling elite of the dictatorial regime. The fountain was rigged with cameras and motion detectors that alerted the guards of the intrusion. They immediately appeared and took us, including our four-year-old child and my Dad, to an interrogation room to explain why Mimi had the audacity to jump into the fountain to cool off, play, and frolic in the water like any child would do.

Traveling through Romania was a challenge and quite expensive. Every time we spent the night in a hotel, we had to reserve two rooms, one for me, and one for him. It was not that we were going to have company or lavish parties. We could ill-afford to pay for two rooms when we were going to use only one. The law dictated, since I was a Romanian citizen, although married, I could not spend the night in the same room in a hotel with my American husband, a foreign national. We had to present our passports each time and receive reservations separately. Interestingly, room rates were double what Romanians were paying. This put a strain on our daily serenity and our budget.

One hotel in Mamaia at the Black Sea was across the street from the police precinct. We were envisioning what would happen when the police came to arrest us since I was not spending the night in my room but in his.

We thought we had attracted enough attention from the hotel staff when Sam stayed too long on the beach and burned like a lobster. The only treatment available to us was Grandma's old recipe for sunburn, covering the skin in plain yogurt. It must have seemed suspicious to curious eyes when we walked in with bags and bags of yogurt. Not only was he in severe pain and feverish, we were arguing what we would do if the police would knock on our door.

Only under communist tyranny, from their desire to control every aspect of the citizens' lives, such strife and discomfort would be created between husband and wife.

Food was always a bone of contention in our marriage. I approached grocery shopping as a list of things I wanted to cook for the week. He shopped for food based on perceived basic needs.

Having been a farmer's son, an abundance of food came from the fields, canning, farm animals, and other farmer's markets. Luxuries came from the store. I grew up as a city girl and our food was scarce most of the time. On every grocery trip, I picked up extras, as if next time the shelves would be empty. This angered my husband as he thought these groceries unnecessary lavish spending. Money was always better kept in the bank as opposed to being spent regardless of the current family needs. Saving was more important, even if it meant doing without basic needs. Money in the bank meant security and peace of mind although the stomach might be empty and growling.

Saving money was sacrosanct and solely decided by the husband - generations of Johnsons have done so quite successfully. Women were not capable enough to make financial decisions or attend college. Leaving finance up to women was derisive and degrading to a man since it indicated loss of control over his family. Women in Romania had more authority in the home, dictated by necessity, poverty, and need. Spouses made collective decisions involving all family matters.

We were poor in Romania and, if we had extra money, we were hard-pressed to save it in the only existing bank, the National Bank, knowing that the government could step in at any time and confiscate our savings.

Inflation was not an issue since the government subsidized prices for food and housing in order to keep the population under control.

Shortages of most basic things meant that each family kept a lot of cash on hand in order to spend it on short notice on perceived future needs, not necessarily current ones.

Hoarding was encouraged and desired as it provided a safety net for the very real possibility of famine. Thus, our opposing views on saving became a source of distress at times.

Living for the moment to me, as a survival mechanism, was more important than living for a distant time in the future.

"Saving for a rainy day was thus incomprehensible to me since we were having rainy days every day, there was no stability and security of everyday survival. How could one be concerned with the future when the present was so dim?

When we started having children, a new can of worms opened. I wanted to baptize our daughters in the orthodox religion. That posed a problem since the deep south did not have any such churches for hundreds of miles.

To make matters worse, my new family considered orthodox a non-religion and a cult. I was thus pagan; they viewed Baptists as the only children of God.

A suitable compromise was found and our daughters joined the Church of Scotland; both were baptized Presbyterians. I fully expected them to chose their own faith as they matured. Mimi and April embraced the Church of Scotland during college and became regulars while singing in the choir as alto and soprano. The parishioners adored the Johnson sisters and their wonderful voices, a blessed gift from God.

My mother-in-law expected us to re-marry in the Baptist faith in order for our children to be recognized as legitimate heirs. This prospect gave me great pause since we had already married twice, once in a civil ceremony for the sake of the government and once in the Orthodox Church, for the sake of our family and our faith. A third marriage to the same man?

We compromised. My husband Sam was the descendant of a famous Scottish clan, and he chose the Church of Scotland. We attended various churches in the area, singing in the choir, enjoying prayers and the fellowship with other parishioners. I was elated when my daughters were able to choose for themselves later on in life. For the moment, the temporary peace and tranquility from worshipping God hid the severe strain in our marriage that could be cut with a scimitar worthy of the Gordian knot. Sometimes I wished we had confession like the Catholics. It would have made things much easier.

My parents emphasized education as a way out of misery, poverty, and dire circumstances. The Johnsons believed that a woman's place was in the kitchen, barefoot, and pregnant. Trying to pursue a doctorate put a strain on our marriage since my husband wanted me to wait until we raised our children, he finished his education, and we had enough money to pay for it in cash.

I knew, time was of the essence - I could be a mom, a student, and a wife. We did not have time to wait. I had youth and boundless energy on my side. I proved it - I finished three degrees in the time it took him to complete his bachelor's.

I mothered my children, was responsible for my mother financially, and took care of the house quite well. I slept very little but I was determined to succeed and prove him wrong. The casualty to my success was our marriage.

I received my doctorate by the time I was 29 but the victory was bitter and Pyrrhic. My doctorate euphoria bubble was burst quickly when, my well-intentioned uncle Gelu, mom's oldest brother, God rest his soul, announced to my Romanian family that I had printed the graduation invitation and commencement announcement in my kitchen.

I could not convince them that young people in a free America could actually pursue and obtain doctorates in any fields. Communists had made it so difficult that only old people were accepted into doctoral study and they had to have the approval of the communist party. Non-members were not allowed to apply. The president's wife, Elena Ceausescu, a woman with only elementary education to her name, in her delusional megalomania, had given herself a Ph.D. in Chemistry.

The worst casualty of my doctorate completion was our marriage. There were certainly many other more important variables but the stress of constant school did contribute to its demise. I did not mourn it just for myself but for our children who were now fatherless at an age when they needed their dad the most.

Child rearing was also vastly different in our two cultures. The Johnsons were strict disciplinarians and punished their children severely for minor offenses. I, on the other hand, rarely spanked my children. If I grounded them, I would soon forget and not follow through with the entire length of the grounding sentence.

My husband took beatings from his dad with a belt and he understood that to be the only way to keep children compliant. I disagreed vehemently and forbade him to punish our small daughters in such a cruel way. My parents had used different methods of punishing me such as expressing their disappointment when I did not perform my duties to required expectations. I would have rather taken corporal punishment than disappoint my parents' expectations.

I spite of the fact that I was the pride and joy of my parents; I was spanked from time to time for misbehaving. Most Romanians had one child on whom they lavished all their love. There was no one-child policy in Romania but that was all parents could afford to feed and support. Sam thought such coddling would raise a bratty child. Perhaps it did sometimes.

Our values in general were so vastly different that I could not fathom why I had married him in the first place.

He loved country life in the middle of nowhere, preferably a desert, with no noisy or nosey neighbors. I loved people, grew up in a bustling city that slept through curfews and lots of neighbors and loud kids. The thought of having to spend another day on a lonely, deserted farm brought me to tears and depression.

Violent storms scared me to death, tornadoes and straight winds were a part of everyday southern life. Uprooted trees and totally demolished homes were unnatural and frightening to me.

Creatures that I had not seen before became part of my nomenclature of dangerous animals to avoid - poisonous snakes, alligators, poisonous spiders and, the nuisance of them all, the huge cockroaches or Palmetto bugs.

Stifling humid heat made everything feel like a hot oven - I could not breathe outside for several months until my blood adjusted and thinned.

The misery index escalated with the soft water that was so soapy, it was impossible to rinse. I was grateful to have water all the time though, without interruptions from the government.

Dinners were strange and ritualistic, with the oldest male presiding over the meal and dishing out insults to women, foreigners, and pretty much anyone who was not Scottish. I am not sure the insults were intentional or malicious; it was just an accepted way of life.

We ate with real sterling silver, a luxury that I found ludicrous and out of place. This was at a time when a complete silver setting cost as much as $15,000. No to mention that it had to be polished weekly. I was so happy to have plenty to eat that I would have used plastic cutlery or even my fingers all the time.

Sometimes the favorite dogs from the twenty big mutts milling about the farm would circle the dinner table for scraps. I found that unsettling and barbaric to have twenty dogs in the house at dinnertime. I never owned many dogs before and found this habit to be unsanitary and smelly. We loved our dogs but kept them outside for protection, not as pets. We kept cats for pets and they did not live the life of luxury either.

Food was very different in appearance and taste and my in-laws were very impatient with me. I was supposed to like everything immediately, and not have any preferences whatsoever. To decline something to eat was a personal insult to my in-laws and to the extended family.

I had an arduous and difficult road ahead of me if I was to survive in this culture, this family, and keep my identity and sanity intact. God sent me salvation in the form of wonderful Christian friends who became my adopted family in Okolona. We spent many holidays and weekends with them. They were my source of inspiration, learning, adaptation, and kindness. I survived and thrived with emotional help and love from my adopted family, the Turners: Lois, Harold, Harolyn, and Joy. I try to repay them every day by returning kindness, inspiration, and help to others in similar circumstances.

Ileana on her wedding day with flower girls

MARRIAGE

My maternal Grandma, Elena Ilie, used to threaten us children into quiet submission at the dinner table with promises of marriage to a gypsy if we talked too much or sang during meals.

Marrying a gypsy was the ultimate punishment since they were nomads and lived, in our opinion, a very dreadful migratory life, full of peril and uncertainty. Who wanted to marry a gypsy, travel in covered wagons, never go to school, steal for a living, and live in a tent? It was dreadful to marry into such an existence. Our view was based on reality, not the distorted, romantic gypsy life portrayed in Hollywood.

Growing up, we were not allowed to date. Teenagers would band together and have group movie "dates," nobody held hands or kissed in public. Only people engaged to be married were allowed to go on dates alone, hold hands, kiss in public, or make out on a park bench.

Nobody spent any time fantasizing about his/her wedding day, Prince Charming riding on a white horse, or where he/she was going to spend his/her honeymoon. It was more important to have a good husband and food on the table. Girls did not expect or receive engagement rings; both bride and groom exchanged a simple wedding band on the day of the ceremony, in keeping with the Roman tradition of the circle of life.

Ceremonies were either civil or religious. The civil ceremony was dictated by the communist regime while the religious one was optional. Some couples chose to do both, on different dates. Either ceremony was binding and the couple received a marriage certificate.

In order to marry, the bride and groom had to be disease free, more specifically, tuberculosis and venereal disease free. Without a doctor's form that testified that neither party had the above afflictions, the marriage could not take place.

There was a marriage house, affiliated with city hall but in a separate location, that performed civil ceremonies every day for a fee. The officer was a communist party member who recorded the marriage, performed a very brief and rigid ceremony, and issued the certificate.

A wedding was planned in advance if the venue was a public restaurant rented for the day, or was a short notice affair if the venue was the home either of the groom or of the bride.

Each family agreed on responsibilities for the wedding, who bought the food, the booze, the dress, the band, the bridal bouquet, the photos, the priest's time, and the two huge candles for the church, decorated with flowers.

Sometimes older brides were already pregnant and visibly showing. It was unmistakably a shotgun wedding, although guns had been confiscated long time ago.

The dowry was deliberated, challenged, fought over, contracted with lots of clauses, and, in the end, if the bride was presented as a virgin and the groom determined otherwise, she would be returned to her family in shame, unless more money was paid to the prospective husband and his family who had to endure such "shame." It was amazing how financial, land, or gold bribes could gloss over any shame. Remote villages followed the old tradition of the bloody sheet to prove the virginity of the bride.

Country weddings were less expensive than city weddings but just as elaborate. Fights often ensued between the drunken groom's party and the bride's party. The revelry lasted three days with naps in between.

More dowries could be demanded and the family had to produce it. Brides were expected to be virgins on their wedding day and potential wars could start when this premise was violated.

Nobody left for a honeymoon; they were usually too hung over from all the drinking and partying. After three days of eating, drinking, and dancing, the partiers went home and the groom and the bride began their married life together.

This is very different from the American weddings since the bride plans for months on end for the day of the wedding, giving no thought whatsoever to what married life would be like afterwards. There is no surprise when many American marriages end in divorce.

The wedding guests brought gifts, crystal ware, dinnerware, household items, but mostly cash. The wedding crier would announce the monetary gift of each person to the entire party. Since announcing sums of money over a microphone was somewhat tacky, some couples preferred that the financial gift be enclosed in an envelope.

I cannot tell you how many empty envelopes I found at my wedding. Why would anybody bother to give us a gift of any kind? I was marrying a "rich" American. I felt sorry for my Daddy who had spent so much money on the wedding of his only child.

There was no giving away of the bride, the religious ceremony was done by four priests in the traditional Orthodox fashion. The groom and the bride had to wear crowns, flanked by two huge candles, circle the altar three times, and recite various religious verses while being blessed by the four priests. The wedding party prayed and sang during the ceremony.

Our wedding was in the Cathedral of St. John, in the middle of winter. It was a cold and luminous day with over 200 guests. My Daddy rented the "Pelican" restaurant for 24 hours to entertain, feed, and booze over 250 people.

Grandma Elena was the matriarch who was often consulted before marriage contracts were agreed upon in the village. She was a seamstress and knew everybody who had girls of marrying age because had planned and sewn their dowry trunks.

She was the marriage broker whom all the families with boys visited and consulted before they proposed to a girl's family. The parents had to agree on a verbal contract and certain sums of money, land, real estate, cattle, and heirlooms exchanged hands before the deal was sealed.

Grandma Elena's marriage broker counterpart was Nenea Nae, the official village shepherd and drunk. He was a self-appointed sage who believed that it was better to be drunk under the bed than dead in bed. This man was as hilarious as he was wise and witty. He certainly possessed more common sense and innate intelligence than many people with degrees did.

During such brokerage deals, some girls were promised to older men of means, there was no love involved, it was expected that love would grow later out of familiarity and duty.

Such was the case when I turned 16. My cousin and I were promised to a 38-year-old bachelor. It was his choice to select which would be his bride, our opinions did not matter or so they thought. They did not plan on two strong-willed, stubborn cousins who wanted to go explore the world. We did not want to get married right away and have kids.

We were to meet him in a restaurant with uncles, aunts, and Grandma Elena in tow, during which time, he would choose. This man was short, bald, not much of a conversationalist, not very educated, and gave us all sorts of bad vibes. We could not leave the restaurant fast enough.

We were not impressed with him or his financial situation. He was very disrespectful to both of us. He owned a nice villa by communist standards at the Black Sea, a Mercedes Benz, and was the Captain of a commercial vessel. He was in various ports across the planet seven months out of the year. The thought that we had to wait on this man to return from his adventures, seven months each year, gave us a great deal of pause in spite of our young ages. We wanted to marry out of love, not for money. The fact that he had the opportunity to sow his wild oats while at sea was a definite deal breaker for us. We did not trust him at all and we were leery of his profession and his demeanor. Marriage is based on love, trust, and mutual respect.

Lucky me, he picked my cousin Cornelia who was a very bubbly red head. Cornelia was not very impressed with this man and told Grandma so. The man upped the ante and added thousands of lei to the bridal dowry/"purchase."

We both told Grandma no thanks; we were going to pick our own husbands someday. We had to go see the world first and make something of ourselves. I found out years later that it was a good thing we turned him down, he picked up HIV from one of the many prostitutes he visited in various ports of call.

Cornelia married a Lebanese Christian, Samir, and had two beautiful daughters with him. Both girls are medical doctors in Sweden. Cornelia and Samir are enjoying their retirement years under the watchful eye of their children.

I married a southern man and we both failed at marriage miserably. God helped me find my soul mate eventually; my second husband David is a wonderful father and the love of my life.

Ileana with Mimi and April

DAUGHTERS

Children are a whirlwind gift from God. My daughters made me richer, happier, and more fulfilled in so many ways. They have been my life and my very reason to exist for 30 years. My blue-eyed Snow-White beauty Mimi with curly tresses received the unique gift of a beautiful operatic voice and perfect pitch.

My green-eyed brunette April with angel kisses on her cheeks received the gift of a scientific mind and a soprano voice. My children played instruments at an early age and were quite gifted with languages.

As an only child, I have always yearned to have siblings. My parents fantasized to me that the proverbial stork was too tired and too poor to fly to our house and drop a sister or a brother.

Always naïve, I searched for years to find a crane that would bring siblings and plenty of food to my house. My parents said that this particular stork took up residence in the Far East and was unable to fly back to us. How credulous and hopeful kids could be!

I never had to share toys or food. It was a good thing because food was scarce around our house and I could count toys on one hand with room to spare.

There were not many material possessions to become selfish over or share. I suppose hoarding food to stave famine was a selfish expression of greed. It happened in some families, within a thriving black market for hard cash. That was not the case in our family.

I decided early on in my life that, when I had my own family, I would have at least two children because it was too lonely without a sibling to enjoy and share with life's blessings.

Communist children, even an only child, were not often coddled or made to feel special. Hugs were rare, public display of affection was frowned upon, and parents did not usually say, "I love you" to their children. I was determined to change that pessimism.

Life was too hard and harsh to spend it on fluff. People hugged at funerals, at weddings, and if they had not seen each other in a long time. Since people lived in the same town or village their entire lives, long-term separation was non-existent or rare.

Three-year compulsory military service for boys created a vacuum in the family unit and a need for hugs upon their safe return and release from duty. It was one of the rare moments to show love and affection.

In recent times, as Romania became part of the European Union, the possibility of employment in Spain, Italy, Germany, and Great Britain, emptied villages and families, breaking up the tight-knit communities, and leaving children almost orphaned in the care of elderly grandparents, themselves in dire need of care and protection.

The far-away parents, earning a decent income in other lands, left children feeling abandoned and bereft of parental togetherness. Some children could not cope with this form of abandonment and committed suicide; others tried unsuccessfully, crying for love and attention.

If there is anything positive to be said about communism, and there is scant little, it forced families to be close, very close, and stay together out of necessity and poverty.

Divorce was almost foreign and seldom permitted. It took around six years of waiting on the disposition of a petition for divorce and often times the answer was NO. However, forced cohabitation of people who had psychological problems and irreconcilable differences gave rise to a lot of spousal abuse, child abuse, alcoholism, adultery, and even murder in the heat of argument or passion. Some people chose common law marriage with disregard for church and morality.

When I decided to marry Sam, my parents were against it for a very simple reason - I would have to leave my home town and go so far away that they would never be able to see me again. Their argument was weak in my mind since I had no idea what estrangement would do to us once I moved so far away from my country.

Being a selfish teenager, I never gave it much thought how my parents and I would feel emotionally being suddenly torn apart and separated from our family unit that had been so close-knit for 18 years. Our entire universe revolved around a 20-mile radius, give or take a few miles, with one uncle living about 100 miles away.

I was too ignorant and young to give much thought to the vast cultural differences that would eventually lead to divorce as my husband and I had absolutely nothing in common. We were as different in our life experiences as night and day. Our only common denominator would be our two beautiful daughters.

I was always told to respect the opinions of our elders and parents in general, but, as a teenager, when it came to the affairs of the heart, I decided early on that I would not listen to my matchmaking Grandmother or my parents.

My Mom had married my Dad on advice from my Grandfather although she was deeply in love with another man, much more educated than she was and Jewish.

My Grandfather objected because his daughter Niculina was much less sophisticated than the man she loved and, in his opinion, he would eventually lose interest in her for lack of intellectual equality. Additionally, he was Jewish and my mom was Romanian Orthodox. Which religion would the children adopt? A very important issue and tataia Christache was a very wise man.

Grandpa felt that my Dad was closer to Mom's education and thus their marriage would be a happier one. Mom talked for years and even today about her first love. Perhaps I was wrong, but I believed my grandparents' criteria to be a false premise for marriage.

I was not going to repeat Mom's mistake. I did not want an arranged marriage, I wanted to marry someone I was in love with, whether he was my educational equal or not, and make my own mistakes, which I did. In retrospect, my Grandpa knew a lot more than I gave him credit for at times.

My marriage was a disaster and doomed from the very beginning, I was too proud and stubborn to admit it. Ignorance and stupidity in my choice exacerbated the problem.

Neither Sam nor I had dated much and married against our parents' wishes. His parents wanted Sam to marry the farmer's daughter next door, so that their adjacent lands would someday make for a larger farm with more pastures and cattle.

My parents wanted me to marry the Greco-Roman champion wrestler from our hometown. This young man worshipped the ground that I walked on and my Daddy and his family greatly approved of a possible marital union. They just forgot to tell me. I only saw him as a brother and childhood friend. We grew up together riding bikes across town to each other's homes.

Divorces were seldom sought or granted in our family but more casual in the west. In fact, I was the second person in a family of over 300 members to get a divorce and quite ashamed of this statistic. Uncle John had a worse record; he had already divorced two of his wives.

I was so ashamed of this statistic that I never disclosed the very sad truth to my Daddy. He died thinking that his little girl was happily married and his son-in-law was taking care of her as promised.

I was not going to admit defeat; I was going to fight to keep us together at all costs. Mom knew the sad truth that I was abandoned with two very small children in a foreign country, to fend for all of us.

She came to help me raise my two daughters and never left. In a way, she is a defector of heart because of her love for her daughter and two granddaughters. From our symbiotic relationship, Mom received shelter, love, and care for thirty years, and my daughters had a second Mom and Grandma who was always home.

I took responsibility for a third adult in my life; it was never easy since she never learned to speak English and could not function outside of home. As my best friend, she enriched our lives and helped carry the linguistic tradition to my children. I hope they will never lose the ability to speak Romanian. Mom patiently opened up their horizons and encouraged them to be proud of their Dacian/Roman heritage.

My mom, Niculina Apostolescu

Ileana during college years

Ileana (front of teacher in dark uniform) with 2nd grade class

COMMUNIST CHILD REARING

My earliest and happiest childhood memories take me to my grandparent's country house in the summer. I spent the first seven years of my life with my maternal grandparents.

When I started first grade, I only saw them in the summer. They were my de facto mom and dad. My parents would come visit me on Sundays. I always felt abandoned each time they left. There was a deep sorrow rooted within my soul that I could not shake until I was fifteen years old.

Grandparents had to step in and help raise a child until first grade, as there was no such thing as day care or baby sitter under communism. People had to fend for themselves the best way they could.

Many children were locked in by their mothers who had to go grocery shopping; others were tended by older siblings. I often wondered what would have happened to me if the apartment caught fire and I could not escape since I was locked in and our apartment was on the fifth floor of our building, with no fire escape. The locks were so primitive that only a key could open the door from the inside or from the outside.

It was never customary to see mothers carry their babies with them shopping or on vacation. Children were always left home with other relatives.

Newborns were never shown to the world for months for fear that they may get sick or get the "evil eye." Superstitious moms believed that someone with blue or green eyes could stare at their babies and cast a spell of ill fortune on the child, which could result in death.

Many children were hurt from lack of proper supervision: burns, scalding, falls, cuts, electrocutions, and bruises. There was some weak accountability but, generally, a person's life was worth very little. I scalded myself and even suffered electrocution by inserting needles in a plug. Mom tried her best but there were no safety devices to prevent a child's dangerous curiosity.

I was an only child and mom did not have many choices. People who had lots of children usually left them with the eldest child who served as a surrogate parent. There was no law frowning on such practices nor child protective services who really cared about the welfare of children in general.

Only when the population was not multiplying fast enough, did the communist party step in and offered stipends to mothers - a form of welfare to stay home and have babies. The more babies a mom would have, the higher the stipend.

Once a mom passed the six children mark, she was considered hero of the communist regime and given an actual medal with lots of fanfare to make sure other women emulated her fecundity role.

Since there was no birth control and no possibility of any legal abortion, women who had been raped would have back alley abortions and often died of severe bleeding or septic infections.

Mothers, who gave birth and could not afford to feed their children, had the option to relinquish parental rights to the government. These children would grow up in the many orphanages designed to raise and educate the dictator's civilian army.

Ironically, such an abandoned baby, raised to become part of the civilian army machine, given up by a woman who had been raped, eventually became part of the firing squad who executed the dictator Ceausescu and his wife Elena. Nobody knows which of the soldiers had the real bullets, but it was ironic, that one of his henchmen may have been his ultimate demise, a victim of his own draconian birth policies.

I lost a friend to a self-induced abortion. Laila was an architecture student and could not afford to feed another human being. She did not want to give the baby away. She was 21 years old when she died of septic infection. Hospitals were forbidden to give medical help to anyone who had life and death injuries from botched or spontaneous abortions.

Women who chose to have babies and worked were rewarded with weeks and months of maternity leave, before and after a baby was born. For the first three years of a baby's life, each mother had generous full paid leave if the baby was ill, premature, or had developmental issues.

Some women took advantage of the system and pretended that their babies were sick in order to stay home and receive full pay. There was a cottage industry of dishonest pediatricians who wrote and sold excuses to justify the mothers' absence from work. It was a disgrace and it created a class of cheaters who were a drain on the rest of society.

Country people had more children because they needed help in the fields. They had an easier life since they raised their own food and did not have to wait for government handouts or meager salaries.

The government did not fuss much over the welfare of children except in the initial stages of adoption by childless couples.

The process of adoption was quite complicated and bureaucratic but the regime lost interest shortly after a baby was placed and a few visits were made to the new home. Abuse or even cases of murder by adoptive parents were seldom investigated thoroughly; the guilty seldom went to jail, or actually served harsh sentences.

Life in general was cheap and expendable. People were more likely to do hard time for their political views or sexual orientation than for taking an innocent life. Investigations were quite commonly botched, files misplaced, evidence lost, or never collected in the first place. This made the job of a judge quite impossible. Not that they were that honest to begin with, they were stooges for the government and thus bought and bribed.

When a child made it to the first grade, life had not been that easy. Parents managed to scrounge enough money to buy supplies for school and the government provided the textbooks and free communist indoctrination.

Everything was taught by rote memorization. Labs were too expensive to provide experiments for chemistry, biology, or physics classes. Visuals or films did not exist, just your imagination. Exceptionalism was always discouraged unless it involved gymnastics. Children deemed promising were taken away from their parents at a very young age and sent to specialized gymnastics centers where they trained 8 hours a day for competition.

Concepts were illustrated on paper, if you understood them fine, if not, too bad. Students did not have calculators, they were provided with an abacus in first grade. All advanced mathematical calculations had to be done with pen and paper.

Parents spanked their children and the law allowed teachers and administrators to give corporal punishment without witnesses.

There was no breakfast or lunch at school. The daily schedule ran for elementary kids from 7 a.m. - 12 p.m. and for high school from 1-6 p.m.

There were no school buses and kids had to learn to walk to school in groups without parental supervision. Parents brought them to school every day the first week, after that, they were on their own. There were no kidnappings since nobody wanted the responsibility of feeding and housing another human being when they could barely afford to feed themselves.

I remember walking past a cemetery while in high school. It was very unsettling returning home in the dark and letting the imagination run wild while passing by the cemetery. I never walked home, I ran. Every rustling in the trees, crunching of leaves underfoot were a ghost or gobbling and sent me flying home, my heart hammering fast.

Few people owned cars and if they did, gasoline was so expensive ($9-10/gallon) that cars were kept mostly in the garage as crown jewels. Owners would wash and polish them with so much love and care every weekend. Once a month, or in a blue moon, the car was driven a few short miles to Grandma's house or to the nearest park for a picnic with "mititei" (a type of local sausage) and beer.

Children were seldom included or invited on such outings. If the family could afford to dine in a restaurant once a year (a real luxury), children were again not invited. Baptisms, weddings, and burials were different; the children became the central part. Their youthful presence and joy inspired hope.

The government decreed that each child had to be vaccinated in school and the school nurse implemented this mandate with the same needles and syringes that were boiled every morning.

Kids succumbed to hepatitis and childhood diseases that were preventable but untreated due to lack of medication, poor sterilization, or doctor care. Doctors and hospital visits were free but actually getting treatment was a different story. Everything was so rationed that the doctor/patient ratio was quite high. One doctor had to treat thousands and thousands of patients. There were not enough hours in the day to see everyone who needed immediate attention.

I was one child out of many who fell through the cracks and suffered needlessly. My mild childhood scoliosis was treated with three months of exercise instead of an expensive corset, which the government refused to approve. To this day, I have constant back pain.

By contrast, the children of communist party elite had the best schools, best food, free vacations paid by the regime, best medical care, drugs that were not available to the rest of us, day care, kindergartens, automatic admission to college, and assured visas to study or visit abroad.

Their parents bought favors with hard currency, usually U.S. dollars, confiscated from political dissidents or by selling assets or art objects from the patrimony of the country. Ordinary citizens who were snitched on and investigated for "economic overabundance" had their possessions in question confiscated and distributed among the party elites. The legal system was part of the problem and did not protect innocent citizens. Every communist member who was part of the regime was above the law and lived a life of luxury, deception, and theft - the ultimate example of redistribution of wealth.

Ileana, 2 years old, with her only doll with a chipped face

GROWING UP

My first memory was of a baby sleeping in a wooden carved crib on the floor of my parents' bedroom.

The rental house had a small kitchen and bathroom down the hallway. It was always cold - I cannot remember a time when I felt really warm except at my grandparents' house when they built a strong wood fire.

Daddy used to blow warm air directly into my little hands and rub them together to warm them. We did not know which family the government had confiscated this home from, or where they lived. We were grateful to have it.

Daddy paid a meager rent to the communist party each month. A small muddy yard surrounded the house and a decaying, broken fence.

Having a lawn was a luxury that nobody could afford and cutting annoying, tall grass was a chore executed with a scythe. Nobody had heard of lawnmowers. Grass grew wild in patches and the yard looked pitiful.

Anemic 40 W bulbs lit up each room. We considered ourselves lucky if the power stayed on continuously. Heat was delivered through steam radiators willy-nilly. We never knew when the plant would cut off our supply of steam and the house would be so cold, I could see my breath.

Grandma had made us heavy wool comforters that weighed a ton but provided heat during sleep. To stay warm during the day, we had to wear layers of hand-made itchy wool garments. I always wore my flannel pajamas underneath other layers for warmth. We even wore mittens most days because the winters were so frigid. It was not uncommon to put on several pairs of wool socks on top of each other to keep our feet warm.

I always loved Grandma's house because she could build a fire. Grandpa kept a steady supply of chopped wood and the ducts of the wood burning stove carried the warm air throughout the modest home. Her entire house was the size of a small studio apartment and built of mud bricks.

The kitchen was outside, with a separate entrance, and the outhouse was in the back, close to the tool shed.

Grandpa had an awning where he repaired bicycles and motorcycles. I was always fascinated watching him make spare parts from junk. McGyver would have been proud.

Because my parents were so poor and unprepared to care for an infant, I was sent to live with my maternal grandparents. My separation anxiety was severe but they had no other choice.

During summers, I would alternate homes and spend time at my paternal Grandmother's home in the mountains. Life was more difficult there and full of extra challenges.

Water shortages were chronic. There was no such thing as bathing unless we took a dip in the river. Women climbed a mile or more to get water for cooking, balancing two buckets on their shoulders.

We washed our clothes in the river or in a tiny wooden tub. We were not very clean, that is an understatement, everybody smelled pretty bad, but, after a while, we got used to it. Changing underwear once a week was a luxury.

When it rained, we were in mud up to our ankles. It was pointless to wear shoes. The overflowing drainage/irrigation ditches became the kids' delight and Grandma's nightmare. The cheap white cotton communist-issue underwear turned brown and stretchy permanently.

Grandma got so mad when we waded in muddy water. No bleach to make underwear white again. She tried boiling them on the stove with detergent, stirring them with a stick to keep from burning herself - sometimes it worked and they got a little bit whiter.

Habits always die hard, I still have a bamboo stick to this day, and I stuff wet clothes into the washing machine with it. It is 32 years old. My husband David threatens to throw it away once in a while.

Uncle Tache, who worked for a detergent factory for 40 years, "supplied" the chemicals. It was easy to bring home detergents that the factory produced. Nobody questioned him. Tache was a scrawny man, always looked sickly, but strong as a mule.

His offspring were mutants who never survived birth. The doctors told him to stop having children since he had been exposed to so many chemicals. Uncle Tache had lung issues all the time, yet he was still alive and active. The last baby he and Aunt Nuta had, lived to six months although his cranium was missing a large piece of bone. Mamaia, Aunt Nuta, Mom and I were bringing home the dead baby from the hospital and, while riding the bus, it was hard to dodge the curious lookers who wanted to know why the baby was bundled so warmly in July. If the baby had been born here in the U.S., they would have done a bone graft and the baby would have lived.

Orthodox tradition dictated that we bury him in a special corner of the cemetery since he had not been baptized. I did not understand why an innocent baby could not be buried in the cemetery with the rest of the people.

Grandma Elisabeta was a tiny blond-haired beauty with piercing blue eyes, biting humor, and healthy common sense. She never met an idiot she did not dislike. She raised eight children by herself from the age of 32 after her husband died of stomach wounds from WWII.

Back then, marriages were arranged and she had married a man much older, 23 years her senior. She never varied her diet, she loved beans and chicken and ate it exclusively. Perhaps it was the good genes, perhaps the diet; she never had any surgery, never took any meds or vitamins and lived in her late eighties. Most of her nine brothers also lived in their late nineties.

She was the salt of the land, literally. Her vineyard and orchard were perched on top of a salt mountain. In her early seventies, the mountain decided to claim the top layers of soil and the whole face of the mountain slid down, taking farms, trees, and the livelihood of over 200 people with it.

She had to relocate in the center of the village on a small patch of land that had a few plum trees, a quincy tree, pear trees, and an apple tree. Enticing aromas of fresh fruits mixed with crushed grapes emanated from Grandma's cellar.

Her youngest son, uncle Ion, built her a new house but she was never truly happy there. She missed her homestead and I really cannot blame her, it was a real paradise that the communist collective could not reach.

Her vineyard produced barrels of fruity wine when the grapes turned a golden hue. The house was spartan, devoid of furniture, save for the bed, the dresser, a table, and her 80 year old icon of the Virgin Mary with the 100 year old crucifix encrusted with rubies. The icon and the crucifix were the only items that survived the landslide.

Although her new house had a room designated as kitchen, she always cooked on an iron grid outside under the shed. I could swear her beans and chicken tasted better that way

Grandpa Mihai Apostolescu, who died at the age of 55, long before I was born, had built the homestead when they first got married. Elisabeta gave birth and raised all her eight children in this farmhouse.

Dad told me, he could hear wolves howling at night in the dead of winter. The isolation would have been too much for a city person like me but my aunts and uncles did not seem to mind. They were mostly quiet people who spoke seldom unless asked.

Grandma Elisabeta raised each child in the Christian Orthodox faith but aunt Leana, the oldest daughter, was the most devout. She was a deacon who never missed any event in the village life.

Aunt Leana and her husband, Stelian, never had children of their own, but adopted a little girl from an infamous orphanage where people would abandon children they could not afford to feed and support. She became the apple of their eyes, indeed a very lucky girl.

Grandpa Mihai was not particularly faithful to my grandmother and, as difficult as it was financially and economically when he passed away from war wounds, she was somewhat relieved that the specter of adultery was gone. I am sure she missed him dearly but refused to admit to the rest of us.

Maita, my special name for Grandma, took me sometimes to village fairs across the mountains. It was an all day trek since there was no transportation beyond our own two feet.

People would trade pottery, home-made canned food, honey, wine, liquors made from fruits, especially plum brandy, dried fruits, dried meat, hand-made cloth, rugs, and the occasional carnival ride would give us kids the thrill of a lifetime for pennies.

A rickety bus used to come once a week to take people to the nearest town, 90 km away, if they had medical needs or to sell their wares on the farmer's market.

One of my recurring daydreams was, a fast car would come and take me away to a nice, clean, foreign city.

We were literally cut off from the world - no stores, no doctors, no hospitals, and no emergency access. The communists did not care or worry that the majority of the population lived in abject poverty and unsanitary conditions so long as the regime knew where everybody was and under control.

People were not encouraged to move away from their birthplace unless the government needed them for slave labor or "volunteer" work in the fields somewhere in the country to plant or harvest the crops.

Soap and clean water were very hard to come by. My cousins and I would escape to the creek to frolic in the crystal clear water. This mild creek would turn into raging rapids during rains that could sweep away even the best swimmers. Unfortunately, none of us could swim. Adults did not seem to worry much and some kids did drown.

Everyone owned one pair of shoes but, because it was so muddy everywhere, we walked barefoot as much as we could. This meant that many kids had intestinal parasites picked up from the fecal matter of yard animals.

We had no place to wash, no bathrooms, no running water, and whatever water we had, we used it for drinking and cooking. No wonder we picked up hookworms! If lucky, children would get a disgustingly sweet medicine, the consistence of honey that killed parasites and restored health over a period of months. The suffering in the meantime was unrelenting.

Kids had swollen bellies and many died before proper medicine was administered. The government was unapologetic and did not care. People were so poor and uneducated; they did not understand that their offspring died from lack of proper hygiene. I fell victim to these parasites as well. The medicine did not cure me until I was in my teens. I was lucky because my parents lived in the city and were able to get treatment. Many of my childhood friends were not so lucky and eventually passed away.

Behind Maita's newer house was Uncle Nicu's home, Dad's oldest brother. His six children had to work very hard to provide food and shelter for themselves and the family. I was in awe, realizing that my cousins did not really have much of a childhood compared to a city kid like me.

They had few books, no toys, no radio, no TV, no phone, and, for a long time, no electricity. The only light came from a petroleum lamp. It was not fair but they were happy to be able to farm a living without communist party ownership. Little did I know that they still had to pay the piper in the form of crop shares.

Even the youngest children had chores early in the morning, fed the cows, the goats, the chicken, the geese, the rabbits, and the pig. These animals were very important as they provided milk, cheese, eggs, protein, feathers, and leather. I felt extremely privileged around my cousins since I got to be a child in spite of our poverty. I never had to work really hard until I was eighteen. I respected them for their work ethic but I wished they had their childhood back.

After finishing high school in the one room schoolhouse, all six cousins left the village to learn a trade in the city. The boys had various professions ranging from police officer to businessman, while the girl became a great mom. None of them had very large families, 1-3 children. It always saddened me that the police officer never maintained contact with me for fear of retribution from his communist bosses. After communism fell, I had lost contact with him.

I would like to think sometimes that I escaped communism for an infinitely better life for my future children, and myself not because I was a restless soul in love. I am not sure my daughters appreciate the kind of sacrifice I have made to move to the U.S. and the life they would have lived had they been born in a communist country perhaps because they are a lucky generation that has never really seen or experienced true poverty. If our offspring could live for a couple a months in a third world country, they would return with a much greater appreciation for their sheltered lives.

I do not think any generation since the 1960s has had a hard life; they have been beneficiaries of the sacrifices that previous generations had made. Having worked with young people for the past thirty years, I can speak with complete confidence and authority that none of these subsequent generations appreciate the standard of living in this country.

There is happiness in poverty but there is also misery and unnecessary suffering. Unfortunately, my children and millions of others are going to find out sooner than I thought the effects of Utopian promises of redistribution of wealth coming from the liberal sector of our society.

Nobody was wealthy in Romania, except the ruling elite. I sit in wonderment and ask myself, are the lives of Americans so deprived that they must give up everything they own for an empty promise of non-existent egalitarian socialism?

Perhaps they are so self-absorbed, selfish, narcissistic, greedy, and self-indulgent, that they want even more, and are willing to listen to and follow over the cliff any two-bit dictator who comes promising the Elysian Fields? There is a heavy price to pay when you lose your freedom to choose. The government that is willing to give so much to its citizens in return for blind allegiance, is the same government that can take it all away.

Nobody in my family had experienced air conditioning before or had heard of it. Summers were hot but dry and torrid days were tolerable in the shade. Evenings were usually cool and pleasant.

There was a city pool but the water was not chlorinated and dark green from bacteria by the end of the week. It was disgusting, nobody wanted to swim in it, and when the city drained the water at the end of the week, they found gross things at the bottom and an occasional dead body. It was more sanitary to go to the river to cool off in summer time, fish, or swim.

Most Romanian kids never learned to swim, there were no swimming lessons or teachers, we learned from each other, if we were lucky. Drowning was very common. I was 23 years old and in the United States before I learned to swim.

I went to the Black Sea most summers and stayed with my Uncle Gelu's family. I never learned how to swim there either - the water was pitch black with algae and quite scary. All sorts of invisible creatures were biting at my feet.

We had city libraries but fun and good books were rare to find and stayed checked out all the time. Who wanted to read a lot of communist propaganda? There was quite a long list of books that were forbidden by the communists and you did no dare ask the librarian to find it for you unless you had a jail wish.

Grandpa Christache Ilie, Mom's Dad, was an amateur archaeologist and a skilled mechanic. Following him around on archaeological explorations helped keep my mind focused and my interest in education and learning.

There was a Roman fort at the edge of the village Tirgsorul Vechi, with the ruins of an Orthodox Church on top. The archaeological digs were supervised by grandpa's friend, Nicolae. The highlight of my day was to follow both of them and observe everything they did. It was fascinating to watch them find a Roman child's sarcophagus with the intact skeleton, reddish hair, and bits of clothing, Roman gold and silver coins, and precious jewels.

Grandpa Christache was probably one of the few men in Romania with access to National Geographic in the early seventies. I remember falling in love with the glossy photographs although I could read no English whatsoever.

These magazines were brought in by a crew from the United States who received college credit at a southern university to help with the Roman dig. I knew I wanted to see these marvelous places with my own eyes. I could not read English yet, but I was determined to learn later in school.

I remember seeing glossy pictures of Napoleon's tomb in Paris and I dreamed to visit it someday. My wish came true twenty–five years later when my husband David took me to Paris on a ten-day trip in December. He is a history buff and we visited Musee d'Armee and Napoleon's Mausoleum. It was cold and rainy the entire time but I was elated because my immodest childhood dream became reality thanks in part to my determination, fate, my husband, and my Grandfather's passion for archeology and learning. I have certainly rifled enough through his coin collection, his books, and his memorabilia.

Tirgsorul Vechi, Grandpa's village, had been a garrison for the German Army during World War II. The villagers were occupied by the Nazis and were unwilling participants in the collusion against the Allies.

The biggest Allied air raid led by Americans during WW II had been 20 miles away, trying to destroy the seven refineries that were supplying oil to the German Army.

One American pilot had been downed in Grandpa's back yard and he hid the location from the Germans until Americans could come and claim the remains.

The Russians had "liberated" the village after the Germans had already surrendered and Grandpa told horror stories of plunder and rape by the Russian soldiers.

The Romanians were more comfortable with the German occupiers, as they were gentlemen and first class surgeons, taking care of the medical and food needs of the village. One of mom's teenage friends had her face bitten by a horse and a German surgeon repaired it flawlessly. Knowing the atrocities the Third Reich had committed against humanity, it was hard to believe that kindness existed among the German officers, but I never doubted the veracity of Grandpa Christache's stories.

A remarkable self-taught man, Grandpa Christache was an athlete by need; he rode his bike to work for 40 years, rain or snow, 20 km a day. He was in excellent physical condition, yet doctors cut his life short at the age of 61 when they punctured his colon during a routine ulcer repair surgery. I say routine by western standards, there was nothing routine about any type of surgery under communists' free care; doctors were so ill prepared, most simple surgeries ended in disaster. I watched him die in the agony of gangrene and it will be forever etched in my memory. As a last good-bye, I kissed his cheek while he was in the casket, it felt like kissing a stone, not my lively, warm, and kind Grandpa.

Grandpa Christache encouraged me to try new things, climb trees in his back yard, explore the environment, collect rocks, make mud pies, dig drainage ditches for irrigation, plant flowers, can vegetables for winter, explore the fauna and flora around his farm, fish, collect frogs and leeches, and be kind to all domesticated animals on the farm. I watched him in awe repair just about anything. His hands were made of gold. If Grandpa could not fix something, it probably was not worth fixing. He reminded me of the enterprising Cubans who still run 1950s Buicks by improvising parts and repairs.

My second early recollection of my childhood happened when I was four years old, playing in mom's kitchen in a large bowl filled with corn meal. I was making "sand castles" while mom was preparing the traditional "mamaliga" made of corn meal as a substitute for bread.

A stranger knocked on our door and told mom to go to the hospital because Daddy had been hurt and was bleeding to death internally. I did not understand what communists were, why they beat him, what bleeding internally meant, and why they would want to hurt my sweet Dad.

Mom dragged me onto the bus, we walked endlessly, it seemed to me like days, and, when we got to the hospital, Daddy was alive, barely clinging to life. I cried because he looked so pale and unresponsive and it scared me. Everyone was praying and whispering. I touched his hand and reached over to kiss him. Several relatives guarded him around the clock until he was out of danger. After two weeks of hospitalization, Dad was released on the promise to eat well and stay out of trouble.

Romanian chicken coup

PETS

I had lots of pets as I was growing up, geese, dogs, cats, rabbits, chicken, cows, pigs, and horses. None of them fell in the category of house pets. They lived around the yard. Some ventured inside the family room, but were never allowed to spend the night inside grandma Elena's house.

The closest pets or pests, depending on your viewpoint, who slept and lived with us, were fleas that colonized her beds, our clothes, and her rugs. We were constantly flea bitten; my skin looked like the canvas of a flea artist. The sheets and the nightgowns were covered in blood from the numerous bites suffered during the night.

Occasionally, Mamaia, as I called Grandma Elena, would get serious about flea control and spray DDT. They died for a while until the eight cats or so hanging around the house would track them in again, carrying a myriad of newborn babies.

DDT was widely used but was eventually banned in the U.S. and production ceased. The strong liberal movement in the U.S. contributed largely to its ban. That did not stop Romanians from using DDT because they had stockpiled it for decades.

DDT was an effective chemical against malaria-carrying mosquitoes but the liberal activists in Hollywood and Rachel Carson's book, "Silent Spring," pretty much destroyed DDT through clever campaigns, well-funded ads, and lobbyists who complained about environmental disaster, mutation, and cancer. Mosquitoes thrived and malaria returned with a vengeance. Three million people a year, worldwide, die of malaria because none of the other chemicals used are as effective in controlling the mosquitoes that carry this dreadful disease.

Recently, several Hollywood stars have broadcast commercials asking Americans to help the third world population affected by malaria. The very people who caused the DDT ban and the spread of malaria are now asking for help with medical treatment. What a sad situation!

There were no vets to care for our pets, give shots, special food, special diet, or treatment for wounds. Cats and dogs had to be resilient, learn to live with injuries, lick them and make them better, or kick the bucket. Surprisingly, in spite of utter neglect, cats and dogs lived longer lives than most pampered pets in the U.S.

We had large animal vets to treat cows, horses, donkeys, goats, pigs, and sheep. Even they were not exactly living it up at Club Med. I remember at least four pigs that had to be put to sleep because of trichinosis.

The vet tech was called on special occasions, when large animals were sick, had stopped eating, or had a difficult birth, such as a cow with a breech birth, and breaking the calf's anklebone. The bone never healed and the vet had to put it to sleep. I cried because I bottle fed the calf and named him. It was a bitter pill to swallow, losing my charge. To this day, I cannot eat any type of beef.

Pets had to fend for themselves in the bitter cold of winter. Dogs had a doghouse with old raggedy blankets on the dirt floor and nothing else. Some were chained to their house and barked furiously, trying to escape. One relative kept killing dogs with neglect. They would freeze to death or die of starvation and thirst. I wished, we had a pet police to punish abusers.

Cats had much better lives; they could sleep in the attic. It was quite cozy in the midst of dry, warm hay and lots of rats and mice.

Chicken, ducks, cows, pigs, goats, sheep, and horses were huddled in the barn where temperatures were milder than outside.

Mamaia would bring the newborn calf, goat, or sheep in the house for a few days, then return it to its mother.

My Bogart, a Snow Shoe Siamese cat, lives like a king by comparison. We fuss over kitty litter, a warm house, and a warm cat bed, and wool rugs, yearly trips to the vet for shots, and medical treatment for the many scrapes he gets from the altercations with animals crossing his territorial domain. He certainly does not have to suffer from flea infestations and neither do we. Are we more humane? People do what they have to do in order to survive.

Grandma Elena's chicken coup (my daughter Mimi in 1985)

Surviving on table scraps, most cats and dogs were mangy looking, yet somehow they survived accidents or diseases. I suppose the lack of vehicles on the road spared many animals an early death. Slow moving wagons pulled by oxen or horses gave them the opportunity to run away and cross the road safely.

Pet store food, or any packaged food for animals was non-existent. People could barely afford to feed themselves, house pets had to be resilient and hunt.

Farmers were very utilitarian when killing animals for their fur. They used pelts to make warm clothing and hats, and processed their meat for food. There was no PETA to force or shame them into giving up slaughtering an animal when survival and warmth were at stake.

The one shameful story makes my skin cringe. The village had a pit where all unwanted pups and kittens were dumped as soon as they were born. The hole was so deep, nobody crawled out and no food or water was delivered. I can still hear the howls and faint meows of despair, hunger, and pain. I was just a kid when I realized what they were doing. I cried for days begging Grandpa to deliver food and to put a stop to it. I hoped he could convince the village elders to find a more humane way to deal with unwanted pets. Spaying and neutering were impossible and too expensive. People were poor and primitive in their mentality. I would go and throw food into the hole but they died of thirst first. Runaways were lucky - their babies were safe from the hellhole.

Romania was admitted to the European Union on January 1, 2007. Prior to the adherence, many written and unwritten laws had to be changed. Cruelty to animals was redressed in cities by allowing feral dogs and cats to multiply to the point where herds roamed the streets out of control.

Dogs became more than a nuisance, attacking small children on a regular basis, maiming many, killing some, and even injuring adults. One such vicious attack killed a Japanese businessman in downtown Bucharest, while he was attempting to enter his high-rise apartment building. His femoral vein was torn by the vicious bite and he bled to death.

It was commonplace to see a feral cat or dog enter a department store or grocery store looking for food. People shrugged their shoulders. PETA had made its way into Romania, and no more dogs were put to sleep. Consequently, they multiplied wildly, as no veterinarian euthanasia was allowed. Country folks continued their cruel traditions unchecked.

Rats and mice had a plentiful life on the farm. They had corn and wheat in the attic and plenty of food in the cellar. They burrowed between the walls and made their way to the attic. On any given night, there was a concert of tapping feet, going back and forth inside the walls, between the attic and the cellar. Eventually the colony of mice and rats grew so large, the house had to be destroyed and Grandpa rebuilt nearby with brick and mortar, a much nicer home.

Grandma Elena's water pump (with great-granddaughter Mimi)

Grandpa Cristache's shed with view of the garden

Ileana, 2 years old

Horse drawn wagon

TRANSPORTATION

I used to beg Grandpa to take me to the mill on the horse drawn wagon. The 250-year-old gristmill was at the end of the village main road by the river Proava.

A village was a cluster of homes separated by high fences on either side of a main road. Fields of wheat, corn, and vegetable gardens circled the village.

The miller turned wheat into flour and corn into cornmeal. It fascinated me how two large stones powered by water could accomplish such a feat, especially since I knew how hard it was to shuck dry corn off the cob by hand. Often our hands would bleed and there were no band-aids, bandages, or lotions to soothe the pain.

The gristmill had a romantic, medieval quality about it, shaded by hundred-year-old trees. The grinding noise was quite soothing and I used to nap on the ground while we waited our turn. The water wheel would spin slowly, dumping buckets back into the river. Droplets would drizzle into a fine, cooling mist. Picked up by the sun, the crystalline water drops created beautiful rainbows. The horses would poop around us and nobody bothered to clean it all day. By dusk, some workers would shovel the dung into a mix of mud for garden fertilizer.

Villagers wasted nothing since there was no such thing as a co-op to buy fertilizer. Ashes from the stove mixed in with dirt grew a beautiful vegetable garden. The only concession to chemicals made was the DDT sprayed generously on everything.

I felt lucky when I moved to the U.S. and I could eat tasty vegetables free of the peculiar DDT smell. I do not think there was an increased incidence of cancer though because of DDT use. It just smelled bad.

The worst pest was the Colorado beetle, a beige colored insect that had hitched a ride on an American plane, so we thought. It had a voracious appetite and devoured everything in its path. DDT was the only chemical able to control it. Without DDT, we would have had a hard time growing enough food and many people would have starved to death.

My earliest memory of motorized trips was the rickety bus going to my grandparents' village, 9 km away from my parents' home. It took over an hour to go five miles and it was not the heavy traffic; it was the bumpy, deep potholes of unpaved roads that forced the driver to go slowly.

I could see the road running beneath the bus through the hole in the floor. The smell of exhaust fumes coming from every crack and hole was powerful and nauseating. I always got motion sickness. I had to accept it if I wanted mobility. The other choice was walking.

Buses were our transportation if we wanted to go further than we could walk. We did not have comfortable shoes or tennis shoes to help us walk longer distances. We were never bussed to school, we walked from day one.

Cars were out of the question as only the ruling elite could afford to buy Russian made Zils or German made Mercedes, Opels or Trabant.

Trabant, an East German car, could only go about 40 miles per hour, used a special mix of fuel, and its body was made solely from plastic. The communist Germans from the Eastern Block must have had a cruel sense of humor naming the car Trabant, "rocket" in Russian, since it could not run much faster than a lawn mower. There were also Skodas made in Czechoslovakia.

All cars cost twice as much as an apartment and there was a 10-year waiting list. The working poor in the Utopian communist society could not possibly afford any car. The ruling elites, on the other hand, could order any western car they wished, and the favorite was Mercedes from Daimler-Benz. If you owned a Mercedes, even a 20-year-old one, you had arrived among the ruling elite. Russians added to their arsenal of parvenus a dacha, a country house, where they could relax on weekends.

Since gas was very expensive, close to $10 a gallon, even if a person was able to buy a car, it stayed parked on the side of the street all the time. The fact that thieves stole tires, windshield wipers, hubcaps, and rear view mirrors, made it even more expensive to own a car.

Obtaining a driver's license was very costly, close to $2,000 and each driver had to attend driving school for six months and pass the draconian driving test as well as the written one. Slalom on a muddy track usually did most drivers in and prevented them to pass the course. Few instructors accepted bribes for passing scores. The licensed, inexperienced driver would be afraid to take the car out or would become a menace on the road. It was more important for some to own a license than to actually drive the car.

Trains came later, as I became a teenager and started to commute to school every morning. I would wake up at 4 a.m. to catch the 5:30 commuter train to Bucharest, 60km away. It was not much faster than the bus since it stopped at every village to pick up day workers who labored in the factories dotting the landscape.

Most refused to work on the farms as it was back breaking labor with very little pay or benefits. At least the factories offered them a once a year paid vacation to a spa where they could treat their injuries through massage and sulfur baths at the expense of the communist party. Since room was limited, their turns came once every five years or so. Nobody complained because it was pointless to complain to the wolf that the sheep are eaten when the wolf is eating them.

Party elites took bi-annual vacations to beautiful sea resorts, mountain lodges, hunting resorts, skiing, London, Paris, and Italy. The rest of the population could only dream. Besides, no ordinary citizens were allowed to hold passports or obtain visas to travel anywhere. It was a forbidden fruit; the communist elites did not want citizens to see how much better other countries lived and how much freedom they had.

On school trips, the rest of the parents, who were not part of the ruling elite, scraped and saved enough money together and hired an old bus by the day. This was a luxury that the proletariat could only afford once a year. Their children saw the surrounding mountains by spending the day in a meadow or visiting the same nearby museum.

A few citizens owned motorcycles because it was hard and expensive to obtain a license. The rules were archaic, draconian, and people did not like following them. It reminded me of the citizens of Naples, Italy who wore t-shirts with black seat belts printed across, in defiance of the new law mandating seat belts.

Accidents were frequent; people were killed by inexperienced drivers or drivers who did not follow basic rules. There were daily funerals of jaywalkers and innocent bystanders who had been killed in traffic accidents.

Parking was at such a premium that everybody parked anywhere, anytime, even on sidewalks. Parking garages were non-existent.

The cheapest way of transportation was bicycles. My Grandpa rode his bicycle to work every day, wind, snow, rain, or shine for forty years! Bicycling by necessity had kept him relatively healthy until his untimely death.

The communist mode of transportation for workers was the cattle truck. Large trucks with open cargo area could handle 40 people standing, stuck like sardines. The ride was free and provided by the union. One of our neighbors, Costel, had died as a result of a ride to work in such a truck. He lost his balance and fell off at 60 MPH when the truck hit a deep pothole.

Flying was the stuff of dreams and only communist elites had the power, prestige, money, permission, and visas to ever board a plane to leave the country.

Most people never left the area where they were born; they lived and died in the same town or village. It was not just a matter of personal choice; it was forced on them by the constant control that the government exercised on their ability to move to another job, apartment, or school.

The upside of such a controlled life was that families were forced to stay close and keep family traditions intact; it was impossible to become estranged from loved ones by distance but you were never free or able to see the world.

Wagon still in use today (www.mycountry.ro)

Mom, Grandpa Christache, and aunt Nuta

Labor

As long as I can remember, my dad was an inveterate anti-communist. Because he spoke so openly about his beliefs and his anti-oligarchy stance, he was never in the graces of his bosses who had to kiss up to the local communist party organizer.

There was a communist organizer assigned in every workplace, they earned double the salary of an ordinary engineer and his sole job was to spy on workers to make sure they were good communists. He filed reports at the end of each day, which were read and catalogued by his higher-ups.

The amount of paperwork and storage must have been overwhelming in the absence of computers. Staggering amounts of data were put on microfiche. Many dossiers kept on ordinary citizens were released to the public after communism fell in 1990.

This community organizer was hated but nobody dared to challenge him or speak ill of the regime in front of him, except for my Dad. He did not hide his feelings of hatred for the communist dictator president, Ceausescu, and wished openly for his demise. His policies were destroying the nation and the Romanian people.

Because my Dad was on the security police's radar, every time the president was traveling within a certain mile radius of our home town, he would be detained under lock and key wherever he happened to be at the moment, at work or at home. If he were walking in the street, they would take him to headquarters until Ceausescu was out of range.

I did not understand why they would do that, my Dad never threatened to kill him and did not own a gun. Daddy was a peaceful man; he would never take a life much less harm a human being. He regarded life as sacred, only God could give it and only God could take it away.

To make his life miserable, Dad would get the most disgusting jobs to do and would be frequently moved from refinery to refinery - he was a petrochemical mechanic and a foreman.

On any given day, Dad could be swimming in mud and oil goo up to his hips, climbing on poles without safety gear, or crawling in narrow spaces with possible gas leaks. It was as if they wished him dead and put him in harm's way on purpose. Dad never complained about that, and even if he had, they would have ignored him.

His labor union (syndicate), to which all workers were forced to belong and pay dues, did absolutely nothing to protect his rights as an employee. There was no such thing as bargaining contract with rights and responsibilities. Management improvised as they wished, with no accountability. The law was only on the side of the employer, the communist regime.

Many employees stole from the refinery, everybody knew it, but they kept quiet. They bribed the gate guard to let them through with their loot once a week. Workers used stolen goods to barter with other people for food, wine, bread, medicine, gasoline, or whatever their needs were at the time.

Dad hated thieves and the collusive robbery. He said poverty was no excuse for stealing. If he reported a theft to his boss, Dad would get in trouble and the workers would beat him up for reporting them.

He came back one early afternoon all bloody and bruised. His co-workers, angry with him for writing reports on their constant thievery, and with the blessing of the factory director, had taken turns beating him up with a metal pipe. They wanted to teach him a lesson to silence him finally. They did not know that Dad did not scare easily. Sometimes I wished he had, he might still be alive today.

Even the director of the refinery was caught stealing wrought iron fencing. He was going to use it around his parents' cemetery plot. The irony was that his parents were still alive! If you think, he did not get in trouble and managed to keep the fence, you are right. Daddy was beaten up once again and thrown into a pit of metal shavings. The height of the platform was three stories. He hit his head on the side of the hole before bouncing a few times in the shavings. When he hit bottom, the shavings had cut his body everywhere. He cracked his skull and it eventually led to his painful death.

He went to the refinery doctor who bandaged his bleeding skull and sent him home with an excuse – no CT scan or X-rays. At the time, there was one CT machine in the country, in the military hospital in Bucharest. Only the elites had access to this hospital.

Daddy lingered in pain and partial paralysis for about a month and passed away on May 12, 1989, from abuse, lack of proper medical care, food, medicine, and fluids while in the hospital.

Workers' lives were expendable, no OSHA there to protect them. My cousin Emil, a welder, was sent into a low tunnel, crawl space only, without protective gear, and never came out. He died of suffocation. How in the world was he going to weld around a gas leak?

The all mighty communist government employer paid lip service to safety and protection but sent many young men to their deaths without any accountability.

You were more likely to do hard time if you were missing money in the inventory than from killing people through neglect or dereliction of duty.

Accountants did go to jail for missing inventory, by no fault of their own. Many factory directors and managers had sticky fingers and pointed the blame on hapless accountants who could not defend themselves.

Everyone worked from 7 a.m. to 3 p.m. with a 15-minute break for lunch. However, many crewmembers would hide to sleep because there was no incentive to try, nobody would be fired, and everyone had a guaranteed job for life whether they deserved it or not.

Not only would you not get extra money if you worked harder, you were beaten by co-workers for making them look bad. Once the freedom and the reward to be exceptional were removed, there was no reason to try at all.

But everyone expected the thirteenth check at Christmas time, a welfare check cloaked as performance bonus. The communist work ethic was, "they pretend to pay us, and we pretend to work."

Women skipped work worse than men and it was not difficult to bribe a doctor to give a bogus excuse. Aunt Angela missed work half the time and still received full pay. Her illness was laziness and alcohol, not necessarily in that order. And she was certainly not alone.

Production was labor intensive and required lots of employees. Automation was kept to a minimum to prevent massive unemployment.

Agricultural laborers worked really hard, long days to put in the crops, weed them, and harvest them. It was backbreaking work with very little pay. Most of the work was done manually.

Each village had one tractor and it stayed broken most of the time, missing parts, or the operator did not know how to fix them.

The dirt was tilled manually with a hoe, the weeds were dug up with a hoe, and the harvesting was done with shovels by hand.

A large percentage of the crop had to be given to the regime to be sold on the open market, while the villagers shared a small percentage according to the amount of labor and the number of days worked. The collective farm of the regime had an agreement with each villager.

When crops were burned by draught, the villagers were paid with money. The regime provided the irrigation systems via ditches diverting water from various rivers and creeks.

Collective farms also raised cattle and hogs, remunerations were done mostly in cash since the animals went for slaughter, and nothing was shared with the workers.

Each village had a shepherd who rounded up the villagers' cows every morning and took them to pasture to graze. He returned them in the evening. Amazingly, the cows knew exactly which house to go to as if they knew their own address.

In mountain villages, there were more sheep herded than cows. You could hear the cowbells and bleats in late afternoon and you knew the herd was coming home. The shepherd was the poorest man in town but always seemed the happiest. He lived, ate, and slept with the cows or the sheep.

Each home raised at least a cow, a hog, chicken, ducks, and rabbits. These animals provided them with milk, cheese, butter, eggs, meat, and fur. Self-sufficiency was important since transportation to the city was difficult, expensive, and uncommon.

Sugar was a rare commodity and so were sweets. It was a real treat to be able to make your own fruit preserves and serve them to company as an exquisite dessert with well-cold water. During wine making season in the fall, sugar was hard to find and very expensive.

Milk was used to feed babies, make cheese, and butter. Teenagers and adults did not drink milk as it was better used to make other products. Most village kids had never seen ice cream, tasted it, or heard of it.

Many adults and children of all ages were calcium and iodine deficient. Thyroid goiters the size of eggs were quite common among the population and osteoporosis since there were no calcium supplements or iodine added to salt. Thyroid supplements were not part of the medical formulary at pharmacies. Nobody dared to go to a doctor to ask for an excision of the thyroid or of the tumor. Who wanted to play Russian roulette with their own lives? It was less dangerous to live with the deformity.

Many factory workers and villagers alike drank a lot to drown the sorrows of their pitiful existence. Communism was not supposed to exploit the proletariat, only evil capitalism did. Surely, anybody who saw how poorly these people lived could not possibly believe this lie. They had no place to go and no way to improve their lot in life. Citizens were born poor, lived a hard, miserable existence, deprived of freedom, basic needs, and education, and died with hope that something better will eventually come.

CONFISCATION OF PROPERTY

By definition communism implied that everything is equal, from the Latin word "communis," "shared." This could not be further from the truth since nobody really shares anything. A citizen cannot lay claim to a piece of land, valley, or a building by saying, this is mine. A centralized government composed of communist party apparatchiks plan and control the economy. Communism is a severe form of socialism where classes are supposed to be non-existent and people work because they want to, not because they have to. In reality communism is not classless, there is the proletariat, the have-nots, and the ruling elite, the haves.

As a political movement, socialism includes a diverse number of philosophies, ranging from reformism to complete nationalization of the means of production.

As an economic system, socialism plans to directly satisfy economic demand. Unfortunately, Marxist socialism had quite disastrous consequences for the economy and thus the lives of the hapless population.

The government controlled all the means of production, land, and property, and decided how much each profession, each service, was worth in terms of monthly pay. Prices for goods and services were kept deliberately low, subsidized through various euphemistic welfare schemes in order to keep people beholden to the government. Some of the population knew this but they were powerless to do anything about it. They wanted more for themselves and their families, but they were forbidden through draconian rules and regulations.

People had to beg for their very existence and sustenance. There was no incentive to do better, work harder, create more, and achieve excellence because everyone was considered equal. Those who were more enterprising, had better work ethic had to pull the weight for those workers who were lazy and satisfied with the crumbs that the communist party threw in their direction. The ruling elite enjoyed special status in this "egalitarian" society. Fortunately, there were no taxes withheld from pay, only forced union dues called "syndicate." Labor was highly organized, Mafia like style, and forced workers to attend weekly meetings that did not discuss the forced production quotas and the five-year plans but promoted the communist ideology and how it fit in with the latest communist talking points or schemes.

It was bourgeois, we were told, to own anything more than your next-door neighbor would own. It was also your duty to report to the Financial Police anyone who had better food, better clothes, better entertainment, a better car, or seemed to be more prosperous economically. Snitches were rewarded for their loyalty.

The ruling elites exempted themselves from such intrusion into their lives, not unlike our Congress. It was fine to control every aspect of the rest of the country, but taboo to question anything the ruling elites did. If you were foolish enough to question the oligarchy, you had a one-way ticket to a labor/re-education camp.

Confiscation of property under the guise of investigation or safekeeping was quite common. I wonder how safe are now in the U.S. our own investments, private savings, bank accounts, and safe deposit boxes?

The easiest pray in Romania were the gypsies because they lived such nomadic lives, were illiterate, and did not have a permanent residence. It was a matter of choice for them, they pariahed themselves through their distinct life style and separate language. Most gypsies call themselves today rroma. Their ancestors migrated from a northern India warrior cast and spread across Europe, keeping their language intact. They were called erroneously gypsies because they were thought to have originated in Egypt and the name stuck.

Their legendary mobility is best exemplified by the joke told when gypsies applied for passports and visas to go to their annual festival in Spain. Such applications took months and years to process and usually the answer was no, sorry, you cannot go. Finally, the bulibasha, the gypsy king, received his answer of no, to which he replied, "That's o.k., we already went and did not have a good time."

This story highlights the fact that borders could not contain the rroma. Gypsies were able to go under the radar anywhere they wanted because people feared them, including the border guards. Anybody else trying to cross the border under communists, without a passport, would have been shot on the spot and left there to die.

Gypsies carried their wealth with them in the form of wagons, horses, chandeliers, silverware, coins, and jewelry, all made of solid gold and silver. Women were covered in bracelets and chains, their dowry.

Many rroma had their gold and silver confiscated by communist officials, under the pretense of safekeeping, and were given bogus receipts by the police. After the fall of communism, many rroma tried in vain to reclaim their stolen property from "safekeeping". These receipts had little weight in court as they were handwritten, with no seal, or official identification. The police got away with the crime because gypsies were generally illiterate. Their children were never sent to school and the government did not really care, they were the unwanted citizens.

The nomadic lifestyle of the rroma made it that much harder to keep up with truancy. Their culture did not put value on education. If their parents and grandparents were illiterate, it was all right for their children to be illiterate as well. There were few exceptions but things are changing now as more rroma are settling down, giving up their wagon trains.

People's homes and land were confiscated under the guise of collectivization, accusations of being bourgeois, capitalist pigs, too much space for such a small family, and sharing the wealth with the poor.

It was not the poor who received occupancy of beautiful villas and ownership of prized land; it was the communist party elite.

The owners who resisted signing their homes and land over were picked up in the middle of the night, driven around in windowless cars or vans, told they were on their way to a gulag and, if they did not sign over their property, death was soon to follow. People were so frightened; they signed anything to escape with their lives.

My Grandfather had buried his tractor in the garden, piece by piece, he thought himself so clever, but they came and dug it up. A chatty neighbor told the police what he did.

They even stole the clock on the mantelpiece, some policeman walked out with the chain hanging around his neck. Nothing was off limits to government confiscators: guns, jewelry, family heirlooms, carpets, furniture, paintings, clothes, art, sculpture, toys, crystal ware, dinner plates, porcelain statues, silverware, nothing was spared.

The biggest confiscatory piece was the former king's castle at Sinaia, a ski resort about 40 miles north of my hometown that belonged to King Michael, the heir to the Hohenzollern fortune.

The communists even melted gold artifacts from the patrimony of the country for personal gain! To this day, some invaluable pieces are still missing.

People spent years in court trying to recoup some of their former belongings, land, and ancestral homes. Some citizens were lucky and received a token reimbursement for their wealth, some got their homes back, and some received less valuable land as a quid-pro-quo. This happened during the period when Romania was trying to join the European Union and non-compliance with the rule of law was seen as a reason to deny its entrance into the EU.

Romanian officials made feeble attempts and token efforts to return some of the stolen wealth. There are many such as my family who are yet to receive any compensation or anything returned. My Grandparent's homes and lands are still embroiled in battle in court as I speak. Mom's land is being developed as a quarry and the government has sold part of the land to a developer. Mom is yet to receive any reimbursement for the use of her land without her permission or any of the profit from selling it or the rocks.

Everybody wondered how the very same communist elites became billionaires overnight when communism fell while the majority of the population still lived in abject poverty, not knowing where the next meal or euro to pay the rent will come from.

There are so many young people with vast fortunes in Romania today; they are all children and grandchildren of former communist ruling elite class who had robbed the country blind for over 30 years.

After the demise of communism in 1990, several billion dollars given by the International Monetary Fund for economic development mysteriously disappeared and was never found or accounted for.

Wealth and well-being still eluded many Romanians although the economic system was slowly changing to capitalism. The new government had promised voters that change would improve everybody's standard of living and they would eventually catch up to the European Union requirements and standards.

To this day, Romanians living in the suburbs of big cities still do not have running water; their streets are not paved, and have no indoor plumbing. Outhouses contribute to huge fly infestations and diseases otherwise non-existent in western countries. Each street has a public spigot and the water is barely safe in terms of acceptable bacteria.

Even the Roman Empire had better engineered water distribution systems for their population. It is strange to see people in the 21st century carrying a bucket to the street to bring water into the house in order to cook, drink, and wash dishes.

More disturbing still is to see humans go to the bathroom in a dug up hole covered with a wooden plank just as they did 2,000 years ago. There are Roman ruins in Tunisia that show clearly stone-carved toilets – they were more advanced than the current population!

The inhabitants bathe in the city's Turkish baths still maintained by the government. The corruption that was so strongly embedded during communism was very difficult to eradicate. The government machine complex was too powerful to destroy although communism no longer had total power by 1990.

FREEDOM OF SPEECH

The words of my high school biology teacher are still etched in my distant memory, "democracy has gone to your head." I spent two hours in detention for daring to ask a question that contradicted the communist story line of Romanian history, It angered my history teacher, Mrs. Avram, because she could not give me a straight answer by telling the truth, instead she took her frustration out on me.

To tell historical truth meant that she risked immediate deportation to a re-education camp. Whatever she believed, she dared not divulge or diverge from the party talking points and revisionist lies.

Mrs. Avram was Jewish and thus under much more scrutiny than ordinary Romanians. She was always dancing a fine line. As a Jew who had relatives in Israel, she was a potential spy. In the eyes of communism, we were all potential spies; however, being Jewish was a double risk. Her file with the dreaded Romanian Securitate must have been quite thick.

There was an assigned spy on every street, apartment block, or village. Everyone knew who this person was, usually an elderly man or woman, either retired, or living on such a small pension that they were sure to die of starvation without the extra help from the blood money the agents provided.

Political snitches and teachers were our "thought police." They entrapped children easily in school. Children tend to be more candid and truthful, turning their parents in without realizing that off the cuff remarks made in the home could have serious repercussion and result in their becoming orphans overnight. My parents were very careful what they said around me when I was little. I was very likely to repeat inconvenient truths at the wrong time and to the wrong person, endangering my parents' freedom and possibly their lives.

What is freedom of speech? If I asked people on the street, I got as many different confused answers as I expected. That is because people talk about freedom of speech but have not really given it much thought. Depending on whether you are liberal or conservative, freedom of speech has different meanings for these two very distinct groups of citizens.

Americans take for granted the fact that people can say whatever they wish, without any consequences. Is freedom of speech the guaranteed right to say what you desire without government censorship, is it freedom of the airways, freedom to write against the ruling elite, freedom to speak your mind politely even though others may be uncomfortable or disagree violently, including offensive speech? Certainly, you cannot yell "fire" in a crowded theater. That is punishable by law because it can result in loss of life.

Do we really have freedom of speech? Can we express opinions without consequences? Can we be banned to Siberia? Are we really banned to obscurity if we dare speak the truth? Do we become journalist pariahs like Michael Savage who was banned in Britain for speaking the truth? Few defended him on principle alone, even though they may have disliked him or his message.

Banning is not something new, many famous writers were banned during their lifetime for literary expression and political views. Many were sent to the gallows, the scaffold, the guillotine, and gulags, never to return. Some were sent to the Land Down Under when it was just a colony of criminals. Napoleon was exiled to Corsica. Ovid was exiled to Pontus Euxinus for his writings and his love affair with the emperor's daughter.

You can certainly lose your job if you exercise your right to free speech, many have and still do. If you are in academia, you may or may not get tenure, depending on your views. If you are a liberal, it is a walk in the park. If you are a conservative, you might as well kiss your tenure good-bye. If you are a student whose opinions diverge from the teacher's, you are either assured a failing grade, or you become the mockery and insult board of your professor for the entire semester.

"Hate speech" has been debated lately as possibly inciting violence. British law punishes hate speech harshly but the punishment is one-sided, only involving infidels. The law is ridiculous and it takes matters to extremes, suspending elementary school children for minor offenses. It seems that hate speech is pretty much anything that disagrees with liberal/progressives' views.

Would "hate speech" laws in this country eventually ban religious speech? After all, there are Christian tenets in the Bible that condemn certain lifestyles. Would discussion about these passages in the Bible violate the law and result in a ban, fines, or jail time?

Rush Limbaugh aptly described the new censorship wave coming from Washington, "civility."Conservatives must be civil during discourse but it does not apply to liberals.

Of all the places in the country, I can think of, a university should be the number one defender of free speech. Based on my experience, most campuses are places where freedom of speech is stifled, carefully controlled, manipulated, policed, limited, discouraged, and relegated to a very small area called "free speech zone."

However, to express your views on any topic in such a corner, you need permission from the university, such permission may or may not be granted and, if allowed, only for a short period of time. Students are coached and often paid to protest an event that diverges from and contradicts Marxist/Leninist propaganda.

Political correctness, a code word for stifling free speech, is so pervasive and so gone amok, it borders on communist dictatorship and censorship. Political correctness is speech censorship any way you slice it. Everything is forbidden unless it agrees with the university's socialist/Marxist views. Most professors are inveterate communists. I should know because I have worked with quite a few for years!

I recognize all the slogans we were forced to memorize during Scientific Socialism classes in Romania. These slogans are used across the U.S. at various universities during rallies for communist causes and freedoms that match the progressive agenda. It is very easy to convince young, naïve minds that conservatives and capitalism are evil. Students are pliable and malleable just like soft gold.

Parents are oblivious to the amount of indoctrination that takes place on campuses on a daily basis. They pay high tuition fees to have their children instructed in useful fields of endeavor and, in addition, they get a good dose of brainwashing and indoctrination into the tenets of Cuban and Soviet style communism.

I remember my elation before I set foot in the United States and the trepidation at the prospect of being able to say whatever I wanted without any fear of being deported overnight to Siberia or being immediately subjected to harsh interrogation and communist jail. I say "communist" to distinguish it from the country club jail in the United States. Once inside a gulag, the jailers threw away the key. You either came out a different person or you came out feet first.

A personal friend, Dr. Cornel, did hard time under communists in a lead mine. He labored there for 17 years; when he was released, he looked rather ghostly and sick. Nobody expected him to live much longer.

Dr. Cornel survived his ordeal and lived more than twenty years in a southern MS town. His only crime was that he owned property, a couple of homes and, as a physician, exercised his right to free speech.

It was not enough that they confiscated his homes, his land, his property, and his medical practice, they had to teach him a harsh lesson he was not likely to forget in a re-education camp. His lesson was the hard labor he had to perform in a lead mine for 17 years! What a gravy train of free forced labor for the communists. And, they assumed, he would never, ever utter another word against communism, if he survived the backbreaking work and the inadequate diet. Most people did not survive their ordeal, especially if they had a weak constitution.

The irony was that he became an ardent speaker against communism and was quite popular on the lecture circuit around the world. He received a comfortable pension from the U.S., had a nice home with a large fishpond and a boat. He was very proud of his lake and the Greek statues surrounding it. I knew he deserved any eccentricity or luxury his wallet could buy. Seventeen years of suffering and loss of freedom in a lead mine could never be erased by material possessions.

I learned very quickly that there were consequences for speaking candidly in the land of the free. We had freedom of speech, but, like insurance, if you used it, your premiums would go up dramatically.

Every time I would point out shortcomings in a system and how it could be improved, I would hear the same worn out answer, "if you don't like it, you can go back where you came from." That pretty much put a damper on objective criticism.

If you made a comment involving someone black, you were a racist, not a good label to overcome. An entire industry of "victimhood" evolved around the accusation of racism. It had to be redressed with affirmative action, quotas, and financial reparations. Even today, it is professional suicide if you exercise freedom of speech in this regard.

If we fast forward thirty-two years, we are faced with the harsh reality that we have lost any semblance of freedom of speech. Anything we say is labeled instantly racist and bigoted.

We cannot disagree with someone of different skin pigmentation, we are racists. We cannot disagree with the Democrat Party, we are racists. We cannot be conservatives, we are racists. We cannot be patriots, we are racists. We cannot respect and demand borders, language, and culture, we are racists. If we are part of the Tea Party movement, we are racists. We cannot punish corrupt Congressmen who happen to be black or Hispanic, we are racists.

If there was a place I would choose to be poor in and free at the same time, it would have been the United States. Lately, I am not so sure any more. Our country is beginning to resemble more and more a dictatorship, a banana republic.

I am having communist déjà-vu every day now. Thirty-two years ago, when I left communist Romania in order to live under freedom in the United States, I would have never believed that Americans would be so stupid as to believe that a failed economic and political system in many other countries over the course of the last century, would actually work in the U.S. just because someone in power says so.

This is not entirely a surprise, we have become over time an entitlement society, a give-me everything free at any cost, a nanny state. The mentality, "the sky is the limit, I can become anything I want, if I just try and work hard," no longer exists. It was replaced by the "me, me" generation, self-indulgent, narcissistic, lazy, and bored by abundance and well-being.

I have been first-hand witness to the dumbing down of the American educational system by the very Marxist teachers licensed by the Department of Education, with the blessing of the National Education Association union membership and the blessing of totally oblivious and lazy parents whose only care was that their children received free meals. They no longer cared about the quality of education as long as they were fed and kept in school all day and out of their parents' hair.

Even the most conservative states in the union seldom had more than a few conservative, patriotic teachers amongst their ranks.

Indoctrinating students via revisionist history and the staunch assertion that America was evil, capitalism was evil, and Americans had to be ashamed of their history and their past worked quite well. Textbooks were re-written glorifying Islam, historical events that did not occur, and assigning inventions to cultures that contributed nothing positive to humanity.

We created a generation of zombies who serve as useful idiots at various protests around the country and dutiful and devoted voters. It has never crossed their minds that they are voting themselves into a life of poverty and exploitation by the ruling elite, an economic status quo they will never be able to overcome through entrepreneurship or hard work.

Violence, destruction of property, desecration of the American flag, of the national Anthem, of everything that represented our country for 235 years, anti-capitalism, and rabid anti-Americanism have become the American creed of the young and lost generation.

It does not seem to matter that a large portion of the college-educated cannot find a job commensurate with their education and will not likely find one any time soon. Politicians with their messianic talk cannot create jobs, capitalists do.

Freedom of speech against the "oppressors" is more important than putting bread on the table. Why worry? Uncle Sam and the government will provide for us all. Is that why you spent thousands of dollars on a college education, to become dependent on government welfare?

I recognize the dependence we had to rely on in order to survive under communism. There was no other way, any creativity and entrepreneurship was squashed, literally, under the heavy boot on the neck by the communist ruling elite. I seem to remember this administration using this exact term, referring to the "evil" banks, oil and car companies, the very people who help create jobs and prosperity under capitalism. The phrase, borrowed from Stalin, Marx, Lenin, and Engels, is a reminder of the horrors perpetrated by communist elites on millions of innocent Iron Curtain victims who were starved, worked to death, or butchered by the "regime" for daring to question the efficacy and validity of their economic policies and central planning.. Scientific socialism and dialectical materialism, actual courses taught in communist high schools and colleges, are just lies.

I used to think that Americans were shameless because they had children out of wedlock and society celebrated their depravity. Churches dedicated special programs on Mother's Day to out-of-wedlock teenage mothers.

Men were irresponsible when they abandoned their children as soon as they found out their one night stand was pregnant. Both sexes were shameless in their lack of respect for chastity and the sacred vows of marriage. Why take responsibility when the government stepped in and took care of both mom and infant through its taxpayer largesse welfare programs?

Morality, honesty, and a total lack of an ethical compass have degenerated so far that nothing surprised us anymore, we considered it part of everyday life, and it became PC. To me political correctness is really political control. Have we lost our freedom to speak to political correctness? I would answer that with a resounding yes.

It has to be political correctness cloaked as religious tolerance that compels us to allow the Muslim Cordoba Initiative to build a mosque at Ground Zero, celebrating their victory over the Infidels worldwide, but particularly American Infidels, the most hated group by Islam.

It is not tolerance that is forcing us to accept the final conquest and victory over our lands by Muslims, over the hallowed grounds where thousands of human remains are still buried after 9/11; it is sheer stupidity and ignorance driven home by our failed educational system.

Why would we, as the most developed and civilized society in the world, allow throwbacks who still live by 6th century rules of behavior and standard of living to destroy our planet, following the precepts of their religion?

PROFILING

When Americans complain about profiling, I am reminded of living under the watchful eye of the ever-vigilant police in Romania. There were three branches, the Militia, ordinary traffic and disputes police, the Securitate, the spying police, and Militia Economica, or the economic police.

There was not a clear delineation between duties since any citizen could be picked up by any of the above and interrogated for no particular reason and held against their will without due process for days and weeks. Their families never knew where they were.

We lived in fear of police, they were not there to protect and serve us, but to harass and imprison us. We were guilty until proven innocent and, most times, we were just plain guilty without the benefit of due process.

I was surprised that Americans objected so vehemently to illegal individuals being asked for identification after crimes were committed. Do we not need to know who the criminals and lawbreakers are?

Every innocent American has to show I.D.s in order to prove who they are at the DMV, driving checkpoints, doctor's office, in hospitals, at airports, at the courthouse, in department stores, at border crossings, banks, voting, and many other venues. You cannot conduct any form of business without some form of identification.

You can no longer pay with credit cards without showing you are who your credit card says you are. Credit card fraud has spawned such checks. You cannot enter any building with a certain level of security without showing I.D. and passing through scanners.

You cannot see a doctor or have surgery without proper identification and a photo ID, accompanying your insurance information.

We feared police constantly in Romania. Many citizens were detained for their views under lock and key at their place of employment or at home if an important politician was passing by. The lack of membership in the communist party was seen as "enemy of the state" and thus of the official who happened to be in the vicinity.

People were rounded up on Election Day and forced to go vote for the only communist candidate on the ballot. They had no choice.

We were stopped because we might have given the policeman a furtive look, a sideways look, perhaps we carried bags that appeared too laden with merchandise, where did you get the money, where did we buy the loot, was it stolen, did we have proof that we purchased that?

Maybe we were in the wrong place at the right time or the right place at the wrong time. Each citizen had to carry an I.D. at all times that resembled a passport. If you had no I.D. with you, you went downtown.

This citizen I.D. called "buletin," had your picture, address, blood type, where you lived, communist party affiliation sector, union affiliation block, how many times you have moved, stamps from the police showing that you have registered your new address as soon as you moved in, or, if you didn't, which neighbor ratted you out and what fine you had to pay for non-compliance with the law.

Not that Romanians dared to move that much. You were pretty much stuck where you were born and raised; job or school mobility was discouraged. Every citizen received this I.D. upon turning 14 years old. This was considered the age of emancipation and thus legal responsibility.

The law judged people not on the basis of precedent but on the basis of the law as it was written and approved by the communist government. This law changed at whim to suit their platform, views, and ideology. This brings to mind the story of Caroline, my childhood friend.

Caroline was my best friend in high school and my freshman and sophomore years in college. We were very close, rode the train together to school for two years, and interned in the summer at the Black Sea.

The summer between our freshman and sophomore year in college, we were interns with the port of Constanta, verifying cargo and serving as translators. It was an easy job. We learned very little in the process other than the system of bribery by the ship captains to the port authorities in order to get speedier approval paperwork to unload their cargo.

The port captain often told us to go to the beach and have fun when there were no ships coming in. One such fateful day, my friend decided to go on a date with a Swabian friend from Transylvania, I will call him Hans.

Swabians were Germans (Schwaben) brought into Transylvania during Middle Ages as goldsmiths. There was a huge gold mine at Rosia Montana. He looked foreign and spoke German well.

These Romanians of German origin kept their language and culture intact through the centuries and Hans was no exception.

Caroline forgot her I.D. home while her date did not. After a cursory check, he was let go but Caroline was detained The cops were determined to teach her a lesson in civics she would never forget. The police check happened around 9 p.m. There was no curfew in place after 9 p.m. for young people over 18 years, but people were discouraged from wandering the streets at night. The two were strolling, having fun like any teenagers would do.

My friend Caroline was taken downtown to the Securitate in the basement and interrogated for hours. And that was not all. Because her date was a German speaking Schwaben (his Romanian was limited as it is often the case with people of Germanic origin from Transylvania), he was assumed a foreigner. They grilled her over illicit relations with foreigners, which was against the law and a major offense.

Any contact with a foreign national was forbidden by law. To teach her a lesson, the five officers of the law decided to take turns raping her. These were men old enough to probably have daughters at home Caroline's age. How could they commit such a crime?

She returned home in the morning, in shock. We took her to the hospital; there was no inquiry, no lawsuit, and no punishment because it was the law, the government representatives who raped her. Who was going to give her justice? A totalitarian government?

We remained friends, although I moved to the U.S. in 1978, and corresponded with Caroline for years.

After e-mail became more prevalent, we wrote for a while and then lost touch. I do not know what happened to her, I know she married Hans, had two children, but I do not know her whereabouts.

Last time I physically saw her was in Germany in 1994 - she drove for hours with her family to meet me for a brief reunion in Regensburg. She seemed normal and happy.

She became mentally and emotionally different in the last two years before we lost contact. Her e-mails were erratic and bizarre at times. I do not think she ever received proper mental treatment from her ordeal and never recovered from the trauma she suffered. There was no closure to her rape - nobody was brought to justice for their crime.

Teacher's first day of class

ENCOUNTER WITH ELITIST LIBERL ACADEMIA

My love of learning would eventually lead me to the bastion of intellectual freedom, the American university.

I felt so liberated, having fled communism, where I had to keep my thoughts to myself or risk deportation to a far away re-education gulag. I would be able to express my every thought without any fear of reprisal, incarceration, or death. Boy was I terribly mistaken! I would have to fear death by denial of professorial and professional appointments usually reserved for progressives who were toting the communist doctrine and party line.

My first denial came in the form of a grant offered by the Soros Foundation. As long as I was a certain ethnic background, belonged to certain organizations, or espoused the communist doctrine, it was very easy to obtain such grants. Since I did not fit the template, denial was very swift.

I had no idea who the great George Soros was. This man had spent his entire life trying to destroy freedom in America and install a dictatorial regime, under a world government led by him.

I did not know he was a Romanian Jew of Hungarian descent whose parents grew up in Transylvania. I did not know his family escaped German concentration camps and fled to America where they were given a proper home. I also did not know that it was alleged that he co-operated with the Nazis.

He has made billions of dollars by shorting various currencies around the world. What is shocking is that his family brought him to America to have a better life, free to achieve the American dream to the extent that he did via his hedge funds, and yet he had vitriolic hatred for the very country that protected and nourished him to wealth and prosperity.

Why would anyone want to destroy the U.S. when so many Americans have died defending it and defending other countries in distress around the globe over the last 235 years? It is incomprehensible.

We were forbidden to have any political or critical discussions in the family, to friends, at work, or in school. Everyone kept a low profile and bit their tongues because they knew, some family members were informers to the dreaded Security Police.

The informers were taught how to bait children to turn in information about their parents. Children were so naive and honest to a fault. How were they to know that innocent remarks about their parents would possibly incarcerate or condemn them to death?

The communist agitators certainly had plenty of orphanages to put these children in. The more the merrier! This was Ceausescu's future army of drones who would carry out his communist propaganda and utopia at the end of the barrel of a gun. All he had to do is issue a command. The reprisal was swift and brutal.

The population was not armed. The president made sure these arms were confiscated long time before he became a dictator. He enticed the citizens with rewards for turning arms in voluntarily, all in the name of public safety and the reduction of crime. The less guns in the street, he said, the lesser the crime rate. People complied gleefully. Who is going to argue with the all controlling, all knowing government who had spies everywhere?

Here I was in academia in the U.S., free to speak my mind, but the academia was communist. I was shocked! If you disagreed with their point of view, usually liberal progressive, you became an academic pariah, you were never considered for a faculty position, much less for tenure, no matter how smart, well educated, qualified, clever, or credentialed you were.

The minds of young Americans were being molded and shaped by progressive radicals who taught them that America is an evil empire, and the citizens are bad apples who should excoriate their sins by giving up their wealth, sovereignty, and their country to foreign powers.

I was speechless and did not know what to do. I was free to speak, but my academic career would be over if I dared challenge the status quo.

I was shocked and could not believe that many professors and teachers were members of specialized unions that rewarded the worst teachers for promoting their platform.

These teachers made the circuits of conferences all over the country and the world, presenting worthless "papers" in the name of research. They were very well paid and had extensive resumes and traveling budgets.

The more popular a teacher was on such circuit, the more offices he/she held in a professional organization, the higher the salary he/she received.

It did not matter that they were seldom in the classroom, that they were terrible teachers, or that they did not care about their students' performance, so long as they promoted the latest teaching methodology deemed worthy by the College of Education.

Parents had no idea what kind of education their children received in exchange for high tuition. I realized very quickly that the College of Education was the breeding ground for future communists and that it would eventually bring the downfall of freedom in the United States.

The teachers hired were usually not the best, brightest, and most qualified to teach, but the ones holding certification, a worthless piece of paper that most people obtained if they jumped through the right hoops.

College of Education graduates were performing in the bottom 50th percentile on National Teacher Exams as opposed to Arts and Sciences graduates who performed in the top 50th percentile. However, Arts and Sciences graduates could not be in the classroom without a license, no matter how knowledgeable they were in their fields of expertise.

The Department of Education issued these licenses to everyone so long as they took worthless College of Education classes that did not improve their knowledge in the area of expertise, neither did improve their teaching ability.

A teacher could have a Ph.D. and years of teaching experience in a private sector, yet, without a license, they were forbidden to teach in the public schools. They could teach college with a Master's Degree and 18 hours of graduate work in the subject area. I found this rather strange since in Romania, only the best and the brightest were allowed to teach. They had to follow the communist party line, but they still had to be extremely prepared in their area of expertise. To prove that they knew what they were supposed to know, they were tested repeatedly before being allowed in the classroom..

Sadly, in the U.S., expertise was not a requirement, just a license. As it was often the case, C and D average students would declare their major as Education because other majors were too difficult for them. This resulted in a watering down of the quality of future teachers and thus a decline in the quality of instruction they delivered once in the classroom. Methodology and proper indoctrination trumped content every time.

As a European, I was shocked how little students and their teachers knew and how open, unapologetic, and unashamed about their ignorance they were. I would have been embarrassed to admit that I was lacking so many basic skills in education and still called myself educated, having earned a high school or college diploma.

I kept hearing people stating how dumb and unprepared they were, yet they held college degrees, could hardly write, spell, read, or express themselves in such a way that it would show a certain baggage of knowledge.

There were so many instances of nepotism in U.S. colleges; it was not overt as under communism, but hidden and subtle. A sought-after professor would not sign a contract with a particular university until his/her spouse would be given generous and well-placed employment as well.

Women were slighted in favor of men, and blacks in favor of whites. How was this, the land of opportunity and freedom, I thought, when academia, which is supposed to be the bastion of freedom of thought, was so communist?

The Romanian curriculum had to be approved by the Central Communist Party and it mandated, besides math and science, strange courses promoting communism such as Scientific Socialism, Philosophy of Socialism, Socialist Economics, as well as revisionist history and foreign languages, particularly those spoken in other communist countries.

Teachers were well prepared in math and science and had to excel in communist indoctrination as well. Teachers had to tow the party line. They had to do their jobs; the alternative was a concentration camp-like prison with barbed wire and watchtowers.

Teachers had to compete for jobs by taking a test and then had to be approved by the communist party. Membership in the party was greatly encouraged and it was frowned upon if a teacher was not a card-carrying communist. Awards were seldom given and the workday lasted 4-5 hours, including Saturday.

Students as well as teachers were forced to "volunteer labor" in spring and fall. We had to plant and harvest crops every year for a month. To add insult to injury, we were not paid, not fed, not even given water in the fields. Because the crops were dusted with chemicals and water was not available, we could not even eat what we were harvesting. I felt like a muzzled dog.

We wore our uniforms designed by the communist party and young pioneers (the budding young communists) had to wear red bandanas. These school uniforms had embroidered nametags and identification numbers with the name of the school, should we misbehave while in public. Any citizen could report a student as to what he/she did right or wrong to the school principal. The principal and the dean were kings. It was not unlike the deans and principals in the U.S. who choose and handpick their retinue.

Corporal punishment as well as public humiliation in the classroom were allowed and highly encouraged. Parents had to attend monthly meetings with the teacher during which time they were humiliated as well in front of other parents, alphabetically, if their child's performance and grades were poor.

Many parents would come home and spank their children not just for the bad grades but for having been publicly chastised and criticized for their lack of parental skills and interest in their child's future and classroom performance.

We did not dare go to school without having done homework or without being prepared for daily oral quizzes or unannounced test. Nobody complained like they do in America that the test was not announced and thus unfair. Students had to be prepared at all times. Grades of zero or fail were given for unprepared or wrong answers. You had to study every time the class met. There was no ACLU, no threatening lawsuits, and no blaming teachers for the shortcomings of students or lack of preparation.

Everyone had to tow the party line and the rigorous and rigid rules of behavior and performance. You failed a class; you had to repeat the year - no second chance in the summer.

Teenage pregnancy was unheard of; we only had one girl in a class of 950 students who was found to be pregnant two weeks before graduation in high school. She had to repeat 12th grade during night school before she could get her diploma. The rules were draconian, but they were the rules of the communist party. Nobody dared to object.

As a conservative teacher, I could object all I wanted to the ridiculous communist brainwashing in the U.S.; people in academia gave me strange looks, ignored me, and avoided me as if I had the bubonic plague. Who dares to buck the educational system? It is the way of the progressives and nobody dares to criticize or attempt to change the system.

Professors are dictators of their little fiefdom of knowledge. They hold the red pen over the heads of the students. In addition, administrators are kings of their little red states called departments.

Here I was, in the best, freest country in the world, yet I was among communists again, and, although I could speak out what I wanted without fear of jail, I could not do it because it was professional suicide.

Ileana in high school at her desk

EDUCATION OR COMMON SENSE?

When I was a little girl, having a baccalaureate degree meant something. Although literate, most people were not college educated. Graduating from a professional high school that actually taught a trade was highly respected. Attending and graduating from a two-year technical school was an achievement. Few people attended college in spite of the fact that it was free. There was no shortage of people wanting to go, just a shortage of colleges, professors, resources, and thus rationing.

The competition to attend a university was so fierce, there were at least 10 students vying for one seat. You really had to be the crème de la crème - perfect grades, perfect scores on high school exit exams, and stellar scores on college entrance exams.

Socialism promised equality and free education for the masses, but resources were limited and thus rationing had to be instituted through very tough entrance criteria - only a select few could attend. Often, those select few were children of the ruling elite and thus automatically admitted in spite of their mediocre scores. If seats were left, were then offered to the masses.

People were proud and content to have an eighth, tenth, or twelfth grade education. Each represented a different ability level and professional track. I say twelfth grade because many students were unable to get their high school diploma as they could not pass the baccalaureate exams.

When Mom was young, under the monarchy, education was not free and most college students were children whose parents could afford, managed to borrow, or saved to pay the tuition. Most families were large and could ill afford to send so many children to college. Perhaps one of out six siblings attended college, the rest chose professions or trades with less education.

Villagers had large families - their children cared for their younger siblings and raised and harvested the crops that provided the family's survival. There was no birth control and religious beliefs forbade abortion.

Children skipped school a lot to help on the farm; their education was not up to par and many dropped out of school completely by the seventh or eighth grade. Most of my Mom and my Dad's siblings had to complete their education as adults in night school during the communist regime.

People tend to confuse education with intelligence by assuming that anybody who is college educated must be very intelligent and those who are school drop-outs must be unintelligent. That is certainly not true.

Common sense and intelligence are also misunderstood - one can be intelligent and have no common sense or conversely, have common sense but not be particularly bright. Stereotypes and human values are assigned to all people based on their educational level, perceived intelligence, and common sense or lack thereof.

The wisest sage in my grandpa's village was the shepherd who walked around half-inebriated most of the time, with a happy smile and an infectiously positive life view that astonished everybody. He never completed fifth grade and had difficulty signing his name, it was painful to watch him scrawl his name for five minutes. He had a lot of common sense and innate intelligence.

I've met my share of educated people from prestigious universities who had no common sense, a warped and shallow world view, and superficial knowledge in general. Their only claim to wisdom was the diploma that stated the potential to learn. Sadly, today "common sense is not so common anymore."

Naturalization photo

BECOMING AN AMERICAN CITIZEN

Few Americans give much thought to standing in endless lines or fighting daunting bureaucracy. That is because they are very seldom faced with such possibilities in everyday life. Perhaps waiting at the DMV comes close to what we experienced every day.

My move to the U.S. started three years before I ever set foot on the plane to New York - three years of endless audiences to various vice ministers, police, security police, passport office, translators, notaries, attorneys, and other mayoral officials.

I had to prove that I had no debts, no criminal record, no communicable diseases, mental illness, associations to undesirable agencies and organization; each document had to be translated into English, notarized, typed only by state approved functionaries, and approved and re-approved by state, ministers, and security police.

By the time I finished the entire process, I was exhausted, had no dime to my name, and had lost all my rights as a Romanian citizen. I was literally a person without a country, a "persona-non-grata," with no rights whatsoever.

I had a Romanian passport with a single visa to the U.S., but no home and no ability to earn a living. I had to pay back my schooling although the Constitution stated clearly that education was free to all Romanian citizens at all levels.

I was stripped of all rights simply because I petitioned for a visa to come study, work, and live in the world's freest republic. Unfortunately, the communist dictatorship thought that I was a spy and my motives were less than honest. As a matter of fact, everyone who made contact at all with a foreigner without prior authorization was immediately under suspicion and surveillance by the dreaded Security Police.

When my fiancé's mother came to visit, we had to answer questions at 2 a.m. downtown at the police headquarters. The interrogation lasted over two hours - the cops wanted to know why we did not notify them ahead of time of the visit. All the while, because they controlled the population's whereabouts through draconian block-by-block registration, they knew exactly who was coming and going into and out of the country. My parents and I were taken in separate vans and interrogated separately as if we had committed a crime. Jane and her son Sam were bewildered that their visit had caused so much distress and heartache to us.

Americans could not understand or fathom total control, but we were used to living under constant surveillance and under a microscope.

Our phones were tapped, our letters opened, our visits, moves, and job locations were recorded carefully. Nobody could ever be incognito anywhere on the soil of a totalitarian society. And they were doing this without the benefit of cameras or computers!

We had become a nation of spies and traitors - spying and betraying our own families for an extra loaf of bread, a pound of meat, bananas, or oranges. It was very sad, knowing that nobody trusted anybody.

The survival instinct taught us to accept and circumvent disturbing laws and rules and to keep quiet. People learned to take secrets to their graves.

Was it easy to become an American citizen? Not really. After my arrival in 1978, I lived for two years as a resident alien. I could not vote and had no rights. I did not march in the streets demanding same rights as American citizens because I understood I was not an American yet. I did not wave the Romanian flag in the face of Americans while shouting angrily that America will someday be ours.

I learned English better each day. I had studied two years in high school, but it was not good enough. I wanted to become part of the fabric of this society, to understand it, honor it, respect it, and immerse in its culture.

I did not want to lose my heritage, I kept it alive at home, but I wanted to be an American.

After two years, I felt competent enough to apply for citizenship. I had to study the Constitution, take a test, pass it with flying colors, and be interrogated for three hours by an immigration officer in Memphis. "Was I ever a communist party member? Were my parents members of the communist party? Why not?" He questioned me ad nauseam.

I knew more about the U.S. history and Constitution than most Americans did. I spoke better English than most Americans. I spelled better. I was truly prepared.

The paperwork was very expansive, difficult to obtain, expensive to translate, and the taxes to the government were costly. As a poor student, just driving three hours to Memphis several times a year was prohibitive. I had to decide sometimes whether I paid for documents and gas to the Immigration Office, or for food and shelter.

It took two years and a few months before I was approved and finally sworn in as a Naturalized Citizen in the Court of Oxford, MS. It was a very proud day for me and four years in coming. I was no longer persona-non-grata, I had gained a country, a language, safe borders, and a culture resplendent with a tapestry of many ethnicities, all united by a common language and goal, freedom. We were truly a melting pot, not a tossed salad bowl. What a sweet day, May 20, 1982!

I do not take my American citizenship lightly and I watch in helpless disbelief the demonstration of utter contempt and hatred for our laws by illegal aliens and their supporters, La Rasa (The Race), the Democrats, and the administration who are demanding amnesty for breaking the law.

The foreign flag-waving and the burning of the American flag in the faces of Americans is shocking. The calls for violence against Americans, racial hatred, pitting one ethnic group against another, go unpunished.

The federal government is approving and stoking lawlessness, racial divide, and the destruction of our culture and country. What makes Hispanics more deserving of American citizenship just because they jumped a fence illegally? Why should we reward bad behavior and lawlessness?

There are thousands of immigrants who are waiting their turns patiently, filling out forms after forms, waiting years sometimes to receive or to be denied a visa to freedom. Vast oceans separate them from our borders. Does that make them less deserving of becoming legal residents?

I had to prove that I had a sponsor in the U.S. who was willing and able to support me if need be. They also had to have thousands of dollars in a bank account; the government did not want me to become a ward of the state. Yet that is exactly what is happening now with all the Hispanics who illegally set foot on our soil - they drop their anchor babies and claim permanent residence and citizenship rights when their anchor babies turn 18.

I had to pay for years for the birth of my babies because the insurance did not pay, yet all illegal individuals benefit from free medical and pre-natal care, food, housing, WIC, compliments of the U.S. taxpayers. Why? Should the Mexican government not have some responsibility for their fleeing citizens? They have more wealth in petroleum than our country does, they certainly can afford to institute social programs to eradicate poverty in Mexico or at least pay us back for our expenditures on their citizens.

The Mexican gang violence and drug trade are spilling onto our southern borders and the federal government is doing very little to curtail it. It is up to the states like Arizona to defend their own borders against the massive illegal invasion. It is a threat to our national security because many illegals do not come here for better economic opportunities; they come here to commit crimes and to harm our national interests. Drugs cartels are destroying the southern border with constant trafficking wars.

Our soldiers would have died in vain if we fail to protect our borders and allow illegal immigration to wreck this beautiful nation. We are successful because we are free and are united by a common goal, language, and our faith in God.

THE SPOILED AMERICANS

I never fully understood the term "to be spoiled." To me the phrase had insidious negative connotations, a rotten food, not worthy of consuming, or a bad person on whom everything is lavished and wasted because they are so self-absorbed and egotistical.

Romanians thought spoiled ("rasfatat" is not really a direct translation) meant unconditional love and devotion to their children and protection from harm at any cost. It never had any connection to material possessions provided to a child. I remember the phrase used to designate an only child treasured by parents for his/her mere existence.

American "spoiled rotten," an idiomatic expression, eluded me as it did not exist in the Romanian language at the time. Perhaps it does now, 32 years after my departure.

Language evolves and acquires neologisms and idiomatic expressions over time and Romanian is no exception, it acquired a lot of English words that replaced perfectly good Romanian phrases. "Rasfatat stricat" would be a direct translation, however "stricat" can mean "not working" or, in vulgar vernacular, someone who is of ill repute.

Do Americans really understand how fortunate they are to live in the best country in the world?

Given the level of malcontent among young people in this country, it seems that they are unaware of the standard of living in other countries or the level of misery those citizens experience day by day just to survive.

Young Americans do not know how much better off they are when compared with other nations. They have been falsely influenced by Hollywood's romanticized lifestyles in England, France, Monaco, Spain, and Italy. Although western nations, their standard of living is much lower and their day to day lives are much more complicated and difficult than ours..

As immigrants recognize, U.S. is still the best country in the world to be poor and spoiled in. Americans have no idea and appreciation for their luck to live in such a magnificent country. Perhaps someday they will understand the level of envy the world has for the U.S. and why people are willing to die in order to come here to live free.

My family in Romania had no idea how unfortunate they were because the governing elites made sure they had no connection to the rest of the world. They were cut off from any outside influence except "Voice of America" and "Free Europe" via short wave radio. My dad would sit huddled every night in front of his huge radio, the size of a dresser, trying to adjust the dial so that we could hear the words clearly, without any static interference. The commies went way out of their way to scramble the waves as much as possible but we were still able to receive some transmissions.

We knew there was a better life and a better way in America, "the shining city on the hill." We wished to have a glimpse of this paradise someday and spoke in whispered tones about the wondrous life in such freedom. Dad used to say that he would kiss the ground if he could be there just for one day before he died - he wanted to feel free.

Americans have slowly become a nation of entitlement seekers. Everything they do, from the time they are born until they die, is a right, an entitlement. They say with a straight, angry face and a loud voice, they are entitled to cradle to grave nanny state. They do not care who is going to pay for it, or where the money is coming from, they want it, and they want it now.

Students had grown more and more demanding over the years - they did not just want good grades for lack of effort and learning; showing up and paying their tuition in full were good reasons to get an A.

My standards were such that I was not accommodating any outlandish expectations, you had to earn an A in my class. There were charges of bigotry and racism from time to time. Nothing came of them, as they were not true, but it was a waste of my time, the dean's time, or the president's time, depending on how far the student would go with his/her outrageous claims.

Sadly, our litigious society is willing to vilify and give credence to any lawsuits, no matter how frivolous, against teachers or principals who dare not comply with disingenuous demands.

I loved teaching and most of my students were good. It was a rewarding profession and I took pride in watching them become the leaders of today. But there were always bad apples in baskets of beautiful, fragrant ones.

I parked my car many times in full light to keep it from being vandalized; I was threatened by students, mothers with guns, or irate fathers over deserved grades; I had to deal with mentally disturbed students who had no business being in college much less among people, they belonged in a mental institution.

I taught students who had previously been in gangs, had tattoo markings, yet they had redeemed themselves; I loved touching their lives in a positive way. Such men and women made me happy. God made me a teacher to be a guiding light for them, the proverbial Diogenes' lamp.

Who knew that I could have run for political office instead of being a teacher, it would have been much easier and it would have required less schooling!

It was human nature to be constantly dissatisfied with the current condition, but Americans took it to new heights and exaggerated the reality they experienced. This was true of liberals who vilified society and everything it stood for, negating all the accomplishments that America contributed to this planet. They were intent on re-creating America in their twisted image and drug-induced logic, apologizing for everything wrong America may have done, by destroying it bit by bit and installing a Utopian society that never existed or survived very long - a Utopian society, they've read about in history books.

These were children who were encouraged to dream, were raised on the coddling of self-esteem as being paramount even though they may have failed miserably, children who were never told no to anything, and whose lives were shaped by money and protection from harm and disappointment at all costs. These were children who were given awards just for participating in an event or for not tripping across a stage.

Furthermore, the very young "progressives" who benefited from the "evil" capitalist system, were willing to destroy it in the name of social justice. This social justice, of course, was not meant in any way to include them.

I did not see any people in Hollywood giving away their entire wealth in the name of social justice. They just wanted to give away other people's money. What will happen when other people's money runs out? Whose money will be then confiscated? Did they not realize what "useful idiots" they were? What made actors in Hollywood such experts on socialism/Marxism or environmental science when they were mouthpieces who memorized lines for a living in front of a camera? Most of them were high school dropouts, never attended college, or dropped out after one semester.

Most of the participants in violent protests around the country were spoiled young liberals with a trust fund who never worked an honest day in their lives; they had all the time in the world to organize mayhem and disrupt society who had to work for a living. They were the perfect marionettes to be manipulated by a few very powerful men who wanted to control the world.

Would it not be divine providence and intervention if they were sent to live in the very countries they so admire and aspire to install in America? I am sure; they would change their tunes upon return and kiss the ground of this free country. It was this very freedom won with such loss of blood by many selfless, nameless, faceless Americans that gave them the license to spit upon its symbols. We are the most giving nation on the planet.

America's exceptionalism has been the guiding light of progress for two hundred years. We are a proud and generous people, and an extraordinary Christian nation.

Bucolic village from Maramures (www.mycountry.ro)

OVERABUNDANCE

When I was a child, I had very few toys: a doll with a chipped face, a teal colored doll bed with a miniature comforter, and 9-piece wood puzzle blocks that formed pictures of various fairy tales if matched correctly. This forced me to be quite creative during child play and brought many neighborhood kids outdoors for improvised games of chase, hide and seek, sledding, ball playing, hopscotch, chess, and dominoes.

Poverty encouraged us to dream of faraway places, fantastical creatures, dragons, kingdoms, and mythical heroes. It did not cost us anything to dream. We were imaginative, creative, and free to wonder in the recesses of our minds that otherwise would be left untouched.

When we could find colored pencils and paper, I drew images that my mind created, unencumbered by outside influences. Clay was plentiful and I taught myself how to model it into figurines and primitive looking vessels. I was not going to win any art contest but I had so much fun. Playing with mud pies on my Grandpa's farm helped shape the love of art. I never owned an art book - I admired pictures in art gallery windows and library books.

We did not have Barbies, Ken, Nintendo, PlayStation, computer games, or any electronic gadgets or games, yet we were more creative by necessity. Why did we not create such toys and games like the Americans? Because we were not allowed to be different, to express our uniqueness, we were encouraged to excel, but within the parameters of the group, of the collective.

Standing out was discouraged, bourgeois, and thus punished. A communist society by definition was a "shared," based on equality society, nobody was allowed to be better than anybody else, except for the ruling elite.

Schools made some concession to achievement by awarding book prizes at the end of the school year for good grades. It was the only glimmer of self-esteem allowed. Contrast this to the liberal educational doctrine today to give everybody a trophy, to make everyone a winner, to promote everyone, to social promotion, or risk hurting their feelings and self-esteem. We give trophies if the child walks across the stage without tripping, we give perfect attendance awards, participation trophies, and many other meaningless prizes.

Should we fail to reward bad behavior, bad grades, and bad performance, the legal system is there to sue us at the drop of a hat. We are the most litigious society on earth and spend more on self-insurance to avoid unpleasant lawsuits. Teachers are afraid to come in direct contact with their students, counselors counsel with doors wide open, while principals use witnesses during conferences with parents.

The uniqueness that made this country great, is now discouraged and shameful, pushing children towards uniformity and communism. In communism everything is "communis," as the Latin term describes, "shared." Sharing may be a virtue in the Bible but under communism, it is a misnomer. Nobody really shares anything. There are poor people and the elites. If I demand my "share" of the pie, of the country's wealth, I am laughed at and sent to a gulag.

We were punished when we were bad, our parents were humiliated, we were humiliated, we were held back in school if our performance was not up to par, we got bad grades if we were not prepared every day, repeated the year if we had to, no social promotion there, nobody threatened to sue the school, bad behavior was not only not tolerated, but was harshly punished. We got up, dusted ourselves off, and tried harder next time. Discipline and failure were natural consequences to bad behavior and under performance.

American parents who are enablers of their children's poor performance in school and preposterous behavior in society, are responsible for overindulging their children with material possessions that are beyond the needs of a child and do not promote healthy developmental, moral, and ethical compass.

Educators catch the brunt of parental and societal displeasure for their children's poor performance. Mom and Dad fail to take responsibility for the first six years of a child life that shape who they are and how they will behave and perform in society. Parents abdicate their roles completely and expect teachers, who are often ill-prepared to teach the subject matter to which they are assigned, to also become surrogate parents who will magically change all the neglect and sometimes verbal and physical abuse children suffered in their first six years of life.

Society's flawed solution to "fixing" this problem is to waste more money on education and demand more accountability and longer work hours from teachers, when the fix would be quite simple - raise responsible and involved parents who stop spoiling their children materially, while spending more time with them and supervising their homework. There is only one other country in the world that spends more money on education than we do, Luxembourg, a rich country the size of a postage stamp. And we have precious little to show for our expenditures on education and our lavish, overabundant parental material spending on our children.

DISCRIMINATION

One of my childhood friends was a beautiful blue-eyed blonde, Ana. She lived two doors down from my parents' one bedroom apartment.

There were five people squeezed in a two-bedroom apartment with a tiny bathroom and a kitchenette. She aspired to become a famous actress and, despite their abject poverty, she tried to dress differently and actually used make-up, both luxuries neither her family nor she could afford.

She was looking for some knight in shining armor to save her from her poverty and she was determined to find him. Ever anxious to fulfill her dream, she ran off with the circus five times from the age of fourteen. The police would bring her back every time she tried to run away. Not that she would get very far without a passport. Heartbroken and locked up on the concrete balcony, she would plot her next adventure. It had not donned on her that there was no escape from a communist country.

One day an elegant, handsome African man appeared in our neighborhood. He was hard to miss since nobody had ever seen a black man before.

He was well spoken, knew Romanian quite well, and very polite. He paid a visit to Ana's family and the patriarch, Stan.

We had no idea how she found this man, it was obvious, Max was her ticket out of Romania. He was one of the first students from Sudan at the newly established Petroleum Engineering School in our hometown of Ploiesti.

After a very lengthy and tumultuous courtship, Ana and Max decided to get married. She was so desperate to escape, it did not bother her that her future husband-to-be was extremely jealous, flying in violent rages at the slightest provocation.

Ana had no clue what her life will be like as the wife of a rich Muslim who had an assortment of other wives in Sudan. She did not realize that her total lack of obedience and rebelliousness to rules might come in the way of marital bliss.

He courted and supported her for the entire length of his studies and, when he graduated, they got married in a very lavish wedding.

Ana left for Sudan and we thought, we would never see or hear from her again. Six months later, she returned very ill, she could not tolerate the African desert heat, all the usual tropical diseases, and the harem rules. She almost died, and, when recovered, she divorced her Sudanese husband in a hotly contested split. They loved each other but she chose living in a communist country over certain death in Africa.

Sadly, today, many young Romanian women have taken the same route Ana took – marriage to a Muslim in order to escape poverty. After having numerous babies who become Muslims, a slow but sure islamization of Romania is taking place. Christianity is replaced slowly but surely and made irrelevant.

The Ottoman Turks ruled many parts of Europe for 500 years, taking tribute in gold and food. In exchange, they offered to guard them from invasions, a sort of medieval mafia protection. Pay us and we will leave you alone. This was nothing new, many empires received tribute, including the Roman Empire.

Soldiers and civilians engaged the Turks in many bloody battles in their struggle to preserve Christianity. Many lost their lives on both sides and Christians eventually prevailed. Today, without firing a shot or handling a scimitar, the Muslims are winning through demographics.

We were born and raised to accept everybody, we were not divided by skin color and religion, the word discrimination was not part of our vocabulary, it was foreign to us.

We deplored the apartheid in South Africa and we knew that our society would never treat people with different skin pigment so atrociously.

The communist party tried in vain to teach us to hate Jews but we paid no attention. We had many friends who were Jewish and we loved and respected their customs.

Our parents instilled a fear of gypsies into us, but it was not based on skin color, it was based on their frequent practice of kidnapping small children to raise them into their culture of theft - they needed fresh converts to make money for their nomadic tribes. Their life expectancy was not very great, they lived into their mid forties.

The government did not encourage discrimination by issuing statistics based on race, we were all Romanians. By contrast, Americans love to separate groups by their skin color, religion, age, gender, and ethnicity, deliberately dividing people.

Gypsies or "rroma" were statistically discriminated as a fringe percentage because they refused to adhere to society, remained illiterate, and kept their nomadic ways.

We recognized economic discrimination because we could see the elite ruling class living so much better than the rest of us, the proletariat.

We knew gender discrimination existed because men were always paid better than women. Salary scales were never hidden, on the contrary, they were published.

Women were more pampered at work and took more time off with full pay. They had generous maternity leave, while men could only take off if really sick. Thus, there was a form of benefit discrimination against men. Few complained, however, as their wives were beneficiaries of such practice.

Age discrimination did not exist, everyone was treated equally bad and everyone was forced into retirement at the same age. If you wanted to work past this age, you were not allowed.

As soon as I became part of the American society, I realized that everything was compartmentalized by gender, race, tribe, age, handicap, religious preference, political preference, sexual preference, income, education, intelligence quotient, emotional quotient, beauty, weight, social status, fame, and athletic ability.

Students complained bitterly and justifiably so that their Economics textbooks were obsessed with race, gender, age, and education statistics. They took umbrage with this excessive division of Americans into so many groups. Liberal textbook writers loved to dwell on race-based statistics.

Every textbook I have ever read used discrimination statistics to make certain points and constant comparisons as if we were in a constant unjust race. I realized then the American obsession with discrimination. There was a real industry of victimhood, rights, and entitlements based on discrimination coming from the leftist academics, ACLU, NAACP, ACORN, NEA, the Southern Center for American Poverty, et al.

I encountered discrimination almost on a daily basis, especially living in the south where people did not have much exposure to foreigners, but I did not allow it to define me, affect who I was, and how I conducted my life.

It was not a compliment to be told that I looked exotic. If I sun-bathed in summer time, people asked me if I was black.

If I shopped with Mom and we spoke Romanian, store clerks would follow us around as if we were shoplifters. Some shop owners would go as far as asking us to leave because they did not welcome foreign customers.

Colleagues from southern towns would tell me that I did not count if I was not seven generations from that area.

Memberships to social clubs that raised money for good causes would be denied to me because "they just did not take anybody off the streets." The woman who said this to me was a high school dropout. She had married into money, to a man who owned a boat dealership, therefore she felt entitled to discriminate because she saw herself as financially secure whereas I appeared as nobody's child and penniless because I was European.

If I asked female colleagues about the meaning of Greek sororities and fraternities, which were foreign to Europeans, I would be dismissed with, "you would not understand," she did not want to waste her time. In other words, I was too dumb to understand.

If I asked pointed questions, I was told that this was not how women behaved in the south; they were submissive and kept their mouths shut. It was the men who made policy and financial decisions. Besides, if I did not like the way things were, I could kindly and politely return to the place where I came from.

If I applied for a job and I was among the front-runners, a person of color or the wife of someone with connections would get the job. It was never based on education or ability as advertised. Affirmative Action was prevalent, not meritocracy.

Mediocre students and employees of sub-standard ability and preparation would be chosen at various universities/companies over better-qualified students/employees based on their ethnicity. It was pointless and counterproductive to complain.

The communist regime at least pretended to have written exams for a job by all applicants, and then, instead of hiring the person with the highest score, hired someone based on nepotism. Similarly, the college entrance exam, although very fair, allocated admission based on communist party nepotism or affiliation in spite of lower exam scores.

Did I get discouraged in my new country? Did I feel discriminated against in America? Certainly, but I persevered, I did not sue, I did not complain, and did not threaten anybody. I got up, dusted off, and tried again, even harder. I never allowed myself to become a victim.

GREEN SALAD IN DECEMBER?

I am staring at my beautiful ceramic bowl filled with a luscious Chicken Cobb salad. The lettuce is crisp and fresh green, the cheese aromatic, the balsamic vinegar is divine, small strips of organic chicken, diced fresh tomatoes, bits of eggs, and the piece de resistance, real bacon.

The room is cozy and the fireplace radiates warmth from the dancing flames. There are smiling, glowing faces all around me. I let the moment sink in as I ponder where all this abundance comes from. It certainly is not from the government or my garden, but the hard work of so many people driven by their self-interest of the "evil" capitalist system. Here I am, an ordinary citizen, having a wonderful green, fresh, and colorful salad in December.

Could I have had this delicious treat that we take for granted every day in my former country, communist Romania? Not by a long shot. The ruling elite would be able to eat anything they wanted but not the "unwashed masses." The proletariat was relegated to dried beans, bones stripped of meat, chicken gizzards, or canned vegetables, that is, if we were lucky.

Government bureaucrats told us how much we could and should buy on the market via five year plans that failed miserably to provide enough food, nutrition, and goods for the needs of the population.

Central planning did not take into account demand and size of the population, it was based solely on perceived need and centralized supply, randomly and haphazardly determined by people who had no idea what they were doing, beyond the ideological rhetoric of communism.

There was never an abundance of anything. The best food was shipped to export for hard currency and the rejects were brought to the local markets to be divided unfairly between the large substrata of the population. Luck, barter, rationing coupons, black market prices, patience waiting in interminable lines were some of the variables determining whether you ate or not that day.

The hard currency bought industrial equipment and expertise, to develop an industry that had no chance of flourishing because factories were never run on a competitive model, they always lost money, and were bailed out by the government.

I wonder how liberals would feel if they had to do without their organic food, fresh food, or food in general? Would they change their "save the earth" tune or "capitalism is evil" tune if they were starving? Do they realize that abundance does not just happen, it is not willed or ordered by the government bureaucrats, it is the coming together of many self-interests driven by the lure of profit? We are successful because we work hard, knowing that in the end, we get to keep part of our hard-earned labor. We do not have to wait for the government to bring us what we need because, frankly, they cannot do so.

I thank farmers for growing my lettuce, tomatoes, chicken, pigs, grapes, dairy cows, and olive trees. All gave me the opportunity to buy this luscious salad today.

There are billions of people in the world who work all day very hard, trying to earn enough money to feed their family. Some go to bed hungry, some forage through trash or the jungle and come up empty and hungry at the end of the day. Some till the soil with their bare hands. They are usually citizens living in dictatorships who are deliberately kept in abject poverty and famine in order to better control them.

We are lucky for we live in a free country. Less than 3% of the population feeds the rest of us. It is an unsung profession but highly respectable and important to our survival. They work very hard to provide the fruits of their labor to the market with the lure of profit in mind. It is not evil; it is justly theirs for getting up very early every day during the growing season and going to bed very late at night during harvest. They are unsung heroes who give sustenance and blood to our way of life, the highly successful capitalist model.

Sarmale with mamaliga, a Romanian dish

FOOD

We never had enough food in Romania to satisfy everyone. Often we went to bed hungry. We were skinny and malnourished. Even vitamins were unavailable - the communists rationed everything in order to make ends meet and offer poor medical care to everyone.

They were selling everything of value that the country produced as fast as they could say, "sold." Even old oil reserves were gone - new ones were hard to explore as oil layered through hard rock at depths impossible to drill.

Most food in high demand was exported to Germany and other western nations in exchange for technology and hard currency, usually the U.S. dollar.

We were left with bones and empty shelves. I suppose bones were good for soup, our basic lunch and dinner staple. Bread was relatively cheap and we ate lots of it.

Ceausescu, the insane communist president, wanted to industrialize the country as fast as possible, at the expense of the standard of living of most Romanians. The elite in charge was spared, they lived like kings.

So what if we had to eat bones and wilted vegetables? It was for a good cause, the Utopian socialism. Never mind that everybody who tried this scientific socialism had failed miserably, we had to keep on trying, repeat the same mistakes until we got a different result - a formula for sheer lunacy.

I will never forget my shock when I entered an American grocery store for the first time. I was amazed at the vast choices and availability of fruits and vegetables out of season and fresh. I did not have to fight other shoppers for the last bottle of milk, pat of butter, or loaf of bread. I did not have to get up at 4 a.m. to stand in line for a 7 a.m. opening of the store. I did not have to carry rationing coupons with me. Groceries were bagged and carried to my car with a smile. The owner was friendly all the time and offered to order items that were not stocked daily.

Nobody fought over food, there were no empty shelves, ever, and people did not have to go hungry. Yet I could not fathom why people bemoaned their poverty and hunger, while visibly showing signs of obesity. I never saw so many fat people in my entire life!

Telling someone in communism that he/she was fat was a compliment. Fat meant that they had plenty to eat, they were not starving. Fat people were considered well off, not "nutritionally challenged".

The "evil" corporations took advantage of Americans, oh, my. I believed them to be spoiled, bratty adults, tired of overabundance and self-indulgence, having everything handed to them, while making more and more impossible and outlandish demands as their American rights.

I do not look at food the same way Americans do. I know the toil behind a cluster of ripe grapes, the sweat behind a fragrant apple, and the backache behind a perfect strawberry just picked off the vine. Food is not a pleasure to be cherished socially in a fine restaurant, or with friends and family, it is instead sustenance and survival.

Americans tend to overeat because food is so bountiful and cheap. We spend only 15% of income on food. Romanians and other poor nations spend a much larger portion of their incomes for daily staples of simple food.

I never look at an orange or banana the same way my husband does. He sees a fruit that is either overripe or too green, something mundane that can be bought in the grocery store on any given day. I see perfection, a real treat, something eaten on special occasions, something that takes a lot of work to grow.

The scent of an orange brings memories of Christmas, the Christmas tree candles casting shadows on a solitaire orange hanging from its boughs with a red ribbon, and the smell of fresh spruce. A not so perfect apple, or a shriveled up bunch of grapes were real treats in winter.

My favorite snack was roasted sunflower seeds. They were cheap and plentiful. The only problem was that the purveyors of such fine foods were the gypsies. Mom was horrified because they roasted their seeds in the same aluminum tubs that they washed clothes in and tripled as chamber pots. She invented the most outlandish stories to discourage me from running to the gypsies with every nickel and dime I had to purchase sunflower seeds.

My gypsy treats were cleverly wrapped in rolled newspapers. There was no such thing as packaging or plastic bags in stores, people had to improvise. Even the farmer's market in summer time used rolled newspapers in the shape of a cone as wrapping.

Newspapers were magical, we used them for toilet paper, napkins, wrapping paper, bathroom reading material, to clean windows (the ink shined them better than Windex), blankets on grass, head cover from light rain, origami hat to shade from the sun, protective cover for books, and to shine shoes.

Food was cooked simply with sunflower or rapeseed oil. Rapeseed oil was more plentiful. There were fields of yellow flowers as far as the eye could see. The oil was heavier and thicker than sunflower oil.

We either fried or boiled our food. Baking was rare, usually at Easter and Christmas. We ate lots of soup made from various green leaves in summer time, tomatoes, Feta cheese, cucumbers, green beans, cabbage, green peppers, lettuce, and green peas.

We sliced them up and ate them raw with bread. We did not have salad dressing or mayo. Preparing mayo at home for potato salad was very time consuming and required a lot of hard work. We did not have mixers.

Mom was a master at cooking a three-course meal from one chicken. This happened once every ten days. We had chicken soup, chicken and rice, and fried chicken, all from one live chicken purchased at the farmer's market.

Dad had the unpleasant task of having to cut the chicken's head off out in the yard. Mom had to dip it into boiling water to be able to pluck the feathers. To this day, I can smell the peculiar aroma of dipped feathers in hot water; it would make me gag every time.

I used to hide because I did not want to see the poor chicken hopping around in the yard headless. I knew we had to eat protein to survive but I disliked the way in which the chicken was slaughtered and could not stand the smell of plucking.

Had we had peanut butter and soybeans, I would have made a conscious decision to avoid eating chicken. It was cruel to kill them this way.

We ate more pork in wintertime since they were slaughtered around Christmas. Beef was not part of our diet since it was usually very tough. They waited for the cow to be on her deathbed before they drove it to slaughter, it was too valuable alive for milk, butter, and cheese. Most cows were like pets to me, I cared for them from the moment they were born..

We ate fried fish and sardines a lot, usually fried whole with bones in and heads, and, shock, whale meat. We bought blocks of whale meat imported from Japan. The process of killing such a magnificent and relatively rare animal had not occurred to me at the time.

Grandpa's favorite food was tripe soup. Tripe was the lining of the cow's stomach and it looked and tasted rather rubbery.

Many people considered brains a delicacy. I am proud to say that I never touched this unnecessary risk to one's health. My Dad liked fried livers - I found them disgusting, along with all the organs associated with the chicken or the cow.

During Lent, Mom and I would make eight-shaped sweet dumplings with walnut pieces. It was an orthodox tradition. I asked her why in the shape of an eight, she did not know, it was tradition.

During funerals, the older women would make a wheat/barley seed sweet concoction that would be given to the poor in memory of the deceased. Since we were all poor, everybody ate "coliva."

Grandma Elena's cure for everything was chicken soup and fried liver. The thought of fried liver turns my stomach even today.

My comfort food was boiled potatoes and French fries. As a toddler, I learned that Mamaia boiled potatoes for the pig and I raided his trough frequently to my Grandma's desperation.

Sweets and sugary foods were rare; consequently, few people were obese or suffered from diabetes. Summer time was fruit and watermelon heaven. If we could not buy it at the farmer's market, we went to Mamaia's house - there was always an endless supply of fruits in season that could be picked. In addition, if she did not have it, there were the neighbor's fruits.

Taking food was not considered stealing, as the villagers, with their meager resources, were very generous. I climbed prune trees, peach trees, apple and pear trees, and anything else that was edible. Grandpa Ilie's venerable old walnut tree was off limits - it had been planted by his Grandfather. He saved the walnuts for Grandma's special preserves.

There was a tree not far from the outhouse that produced a yellow berry, the size of a raspberry, called "dude." We climbed that tall tree many times for juicy berries, with total disregard for the proximity to the outhouse. Why would we care? We were kids and ate anything that tasted good and never washed them.

We got in trouble once when picking radiant red poppies in a wheat field that belonged to a communist co-operative and the guard chased us with an ax. I still remember the sheer terror of impending death by decapitation with an ax when I see red poppies. He was so angry, perhaps the poppies were his opium stash and we stumbled upon it accidentally. I can still smell the pungent odor of the stems. Nobody has ever chased us before when we tried to pick flowers or fruits. We were utterly frightened.

My American born children were very wasteful with their food. When they were very young, we took regular trips to Pizza Hut. Half of the pizza was usually squandered after they were full. I scolded them that some children were starving and they should learn to order only what they could consume. With a cocky attitude, my girls offered to mail them to starving children or challenged me to name a few starving at that moment. The wastefulness was lost on them. I found this to be typical of most American children.

We never knew what eating out meant. Fancy restaurants were off-limits for the masses and fast food restaurants did not exist.

Nobody fed us breakfast and lunches at school. The government could not care less if we went hungry, had money to buy food, or had time and energy to stand in lines in sub-zero temperatures for hours.

We ate better and stuffed ourselves at weddings, baptisms, and funerals. Easter and Christmas were also occasions of good eating and over stuffing.

Going on a picnic was reserved for party elites who reveled in their newfound power to grab the best accommodations for themselves and their families. We did not like it but were powerless to do anything about it. Our guns had been confiscated early on in the communist oligarchy takeover.

I can only remember a couple of occasions when I ate out - at lake Snagov with Manescu and his wife - he had money and power none of us could even dream of. Both were very influential in the communist party. The second time I dined in decadent luxury was at my wedding, in the restaurant "Pelican" rented by my father – and he had to spend his entire life's savings.

There was no such thing as spending the night at the house of a friend or pajama parties. First, pajamas were hard to find. Secondly, parties were considered bourgeois, unless you were part of the ruling elite. Nobody in his/her right mind would be willing to feed half a dozen kids at an overnight party when food was hard to procure and families could barely afford to feed themselves.

Nobody kidnapped kids because they were too expensive to feed. You could let them walk to school alone, take the bus, and they always came back. Besides, with all levels of police tripping over each other everywhere, nobody dared to do anything illegal or stupid that would land him or her in jail, doing hard time in a real gulag, not some Club Med on steroids. I cannot remember birthday parties or birthday cakes. It was a luxury reserved for those in power.

I always enjoyed eating at relatives' homes because they always served the best food they had. You did not have to have a special invitation, or call ahead. If you visited close to lunch or dinnertime, the invitation was automatic. It was considered rude to refuse lunch or dinner, no matter how starving the family was, or how little food they had to offer.

Occasionally, my Dad would take us for our Sunday promenade and feed us cake at the bakery on the boulevard. I always felt special, Daddy's little girl, because Dad sacrificed his allowance to buy me a decadent piece of velvety chocolate cake. It was the ultimate luxury for me. There was ice cream in the bakery as well, but it was a rare treat. The ultimate luxury was Profiterole, an ice cream and cake concoction that only the French could make so divine. Americans do not consider a meal complete unless they have had dessert. Communism does not offer such luxury.

Few people owned a refrigerator and if they did, it was very small. It was thus necessary to buy food every day.

Mom, Dad, and I took turns shopping, but it was mostly Mom's duty and mine. We purchased vegetables in summer time at the farmer's market and had to be quite choosy as our food budget was limited.

The state had green groceries but the shelves were mostly empty. Some had a few wilted leaves of spinach or potatoes with worms poking out of holes.

The Colorado beetle loved potatoes! I did not know where Colorado was, but I was positive it was infested with bugs since this fast-multiplying pest had hitched a ride so many thousands of miles away, arriving in Romania on a plane and devouring our precious food. The beetle had a voracious appetite; Grandpa and I used to pick them off tomatoes and potatoes by buckets full.

In wintertime, it was more difficult to find vegetables. There were some canned fruits and vegetables, quite expensive and often inedible as cans and jars were poorly sealed.

Meat was more plentiful because it was easier to preserve by curing it with salt or with lard. My grandparents' cellar maintained a constant low temperature and they stored fruits, cured meat, and salty, smoked fish.

Why did we shop every day for food? Was it because we liked fresh more? Was it because we had no refrigeration? Was it because, if we did have refrigeration, they were small and we could not afford the electricity? Was it because we had no cars and could only carry a day's supply of food with two armloads a long way home? It was probably all of the above.

My love for bread formed when I was six years old and mom sent me to the store with three lei wadded in my sweaty palm to buy French bread. I loved French bread, and, if I were lucky, it would still be warm from the oven. I would eat half the crust by the time I made it home. It was worth the spanking I got every time for ruining the loaf for everybody else.

Wheat bread was round and less expensive - we had no idea that the fiber was stripped from the white bread. We thought the communists were lucky because they could buy French bread any time they wanted while we had to eat darker bread, which was harder to chew. Bread was easier to find but still in short supply, you had to be at the store at the right time.

Grandpa spoiled me twice a year with a chocolate bar filled with raisins. Raisins - it was heaven. They were hard to find because grapes were made into wine; wine production was much more profitable than raisins. Besides, all the winos paid heavy taxes for their drinking curse. Some people even used raisins to make alcohol.

Every family owned a couple of seltzer bottles made of heavy gauge green or blue glass. A refill center would pressurize gas and water into this bottle for a small fee. In Roman style, wine and seltzer were mixed half-and-half to make the wine last longer. Although a wire mesh was cupping the seltzer bottle while being filled with water and CO_2, accidents happened and people would be decapitated or maimed. I thought it a heavy price to pay for people's addiction to drinking wine.

Children would mix seltzer water with syrup and have an instant soda. There was no Coke or Pepsi on the communist market. Pepsi was introduced on the market in Romania in the early 1980s but only the privileged few had access to buy it.

Splitting wood for heat and cooking (www.mycountry.ro)

HOW OFTEN DO YOU VISIT ROMANIA?

I used to be ashamed and frustrated when people asked me how often I visited my relatives in Romania. Perfect strangers, friends, and acquaintances alike were prying into the most intimate details of my life, which I did not have time to disclose in one sentence or two, nor did I wish to discuss in those moments. I did not want to be rude, but, no matter how I answered, people were not satisfied or comfortable. "I'd rather not say," became my standard answer instead of launching into a lengthy explanation that was none of their business.

I am an only child, my dad passed away in 1989, and my mom lives with us. Simple explanation but that leaves out the nagging question of all the relatives that I have not seen since 1985.

Should I have told them how pained I was at the thought of having to return to the misery that I had escaped? To them it seemed like a fun vacation to trek across the globe for 24 hours in a very cramped airplane, sleep in airports, and take taxis and buses before I could even remotely reach a place where some of my relatives lived.

Was it fun to spend $2,000 on the flight alone, to forcefully exchange $30/day for the duration of my stay, whether I was going to spend that much or not? Was it fun to do without a shower or bath for days on end? Not knowing where my next meal was going to be? Was it fun worrying about my safety? Worrying about getting sick and being unable to receive proper treatment or medicine? Thirty dollars was a lot of money in Romania of the late 1970s. Was it fun to spend so much money I could ill afford in order to be used, harassed, and abused by the authorities for the duration of my visit?

Should I have told my questioners that I was a poor student and did not have that kind of money? I wanted to see my parents, my relatives more than anything in the world, but it was more than I spent on rent and food in a year!

I felt poor, wretched, inadequate, and alone. Should I have told them that my children came first, they had to eat and needed a safe and clean place to call home before I satisfied my longing to see my birthplace and my relatives?

Often times I was too ill to travel. Twenty-four hours is a long way to go to reach my destination, with many stopovers and plane changes. When my Dad passed away, I was unable to attend his funeral - I was in traction at the hospital from a ruptured disk. How do you explain the mental anguish and the physical pain? How can people possibly understand?

Now that I have more time and money to travel, I do not have many immediate relatives who are still alive. They have succumbed to communist abuse, neglect, or to the hard life induced by years and years of communist rule and micro-mismanagement of their lives and of the economy. The nanny state with its rationing of everything killed them all - from cradle to grave, was the communist mantra.

Things have changed to a certain degree, the economy is chugging on the path to capitalism, but poor people's lives, which are most of the population, have not. Only the former communist elites have the money and know-how to game the system in order to thrive in the post European Union economy.

A large chunk of the labor force moved to greener pastures to find employment, over 11% of the population - Spain, Italy, Portugal, France, United Kingdom, to name a few. They left their children in the care of elderly people who were themselves in need of care.

Even gypsies took off to establish theft ghettos in EU countries that were so politically correct, they would be able to game the system and steal to their hearts' content without fear of deportation or retribution. After all, they are EU citizens.

My good friend Flor travels often to Romania on business and I hear about the misery and poverty that still exists, 21 years after the fall of communism.

The state of disrepair is incredible; factories have been sold off piece-by-piece, or are rusting in the polluted air. Mountains of garbage are not being picked up, while wild dogs are allowed to run in packs and terrorize the citizens.

Nobody seems to be in charge anymore. Political corruption, theft, and dishonor are the accepted norm. The justice system runs on bribes, the police is corrupt, the banking system is abusive, and the wolves are running the flock of "sheeple."

Nobody seems to manufacture anything anymore. Gypsies dismantle railroad tracks and sell them for scrap metal. How desperate must one be to try to take apart transformers to make an easy euro, electrocuting themselves in the process? Everything has been sold off to foreign countries. Sounds familiar?

I would like to take my adult children and my husband someday to show them where I grew up, went to school, where I came from. They are willing to go but I am afraid, very afraid.

This is my home now; I have lived in America much longer than I have lived in Romania. Yes, my roots were there but home is where the hearth is and that happens to be Virginia. I pledged allegiance to the United States and I intend to fight for its survival, for my home, and my family's future.

Hopefully, sooner than later, we can all travel to Romania and lay a wreath at my father's tomb, my grandparents' memorial, and my aunts and uncles who have passed away. God rest their souls, they were great patriots who gave their all to their country!

Current village home, still without plumbing

GAMING THE SYSTEM

I often wondered how we survived 29 years of communism. We were resilient for sure; the survival instinct kicked in and we learned quickly, as a nation, how to game the system. It was not an issue of moral ethics, it was an issue of how were we going to eat or stay warm another day.

I am also wondering about certain Americans and illegal aliens who are taught by ACORN, La Raza, the Mexican Consulate, the Southern Poverty Law Center, and other like-minded liberal groups to obtain legal and illegal benefits under the loopholes of the law, enabled by many generations of Democrat Congressmen who view this country as discriminatory and socially unjust and thus in need of "fundamental change" that only they can bring about, providing that the new beneficiaries of their benevolence vote Democrat in perpetuity.

People like me, who escaped oppressive regimes, know and recognize that these euphemisms are code words for socialism and communism. Without help from lawmakers, we had to improvise and devise our own survival plans under the radar of the Economic and Fiscal Police. Groups of Americans and illegal aliens game the system in a country where freedom still offers its legal citizens the opportunity to reach the American dream without theft.

The economic barter system based on theft became for some the predominant method of survival and economic exchange under communism. I say for some because there were citizens who never engaged in barter via theft. Their religious and moral beliefs forbade them to do so. They believed in hard work, earning everything they got and being generous to their fellow man who had less than they did.

Many workers (we were all workers to the communist regime) stole materials, finished products, or services from their employer, in this case, the communist government. It never occurred to them that they were stealing from themselves because nobody believed the ideological lies that the means of production were owned in common. Everybody worked for a monthly salary that was very similar, regardless of profession. Only miners and a few others in the chemical field received extra pay.

People knew they only owned the clothes on their backs, dishes, and a few pieces of furniture. Because their communist daily needs were barely satisfied, workers exchanged with others various goods and services in short supply, under the radar of the Economic Police. A butcher would trade stolen meat for a case of wine, a week's worth of bread, a couple of liters of cooking oil, medicines in short supply, soap, shampoo, a doctor's more attentive care for a patient, or a couple of kilos of sugar and flour.

Farmers were more honest in their exchanges since they at least raised the animals or grew the fruits and vegetables. Some lazier and thus needier farmers resorted to stealing, selling, and/or slaughtering a neighbor's pig, cow, or sheep. If they were caught, so be it, the jail time was worth surviving a few months on the stolen meat.

Lazier farmers brings to mind the failed communist experiment at Jamestown where each family labored together for the community but some chose to labor less than others but all benefited equally from the crop. It is for this reason that the community as a whole was facing starvation. They soon realized that dividing the land into smaller plots and giving them to each family increased the incentive to work and thus the successful capitalist model was born. And they were hungry no more.

More daring thieves stole goods made of iron and sold them as recycled scrap metal, i.e., rail road tracks, metal fences, transformers, light fixtures, cemetery rails, marble crosses, road markers, and pretty much anything that was not nailed down, screwed too tightly, or cemented.

Gypsies took theft to new heights in their race for survival. The rroma, the now PC term for gypsies, stole car tires, windshield wipers, rear view mirrors, metal bars from windows, trash cans, door handles, public commodes, toilet paper, and pretty much anything in stores that their huge skirts with multiple pockets could hide.

They stole electricity by connecting directly to the light poles. As soon as they were disconnected, they would re-connect. The government would give up in the cat and mouse game.

When given free apartments to take them off the cold streets and migratory wagons, gypsies dismantled them and sold everything piece by piece, doors, appliances, commodes, sinks, light fixtures, parquet flooring, linoleum, until there was nothing else left but the bare walls. Afterwards they moved out into the courtyard where they slept around huge campfires and improvised tents.

Gaming the system also involved birthing multiple babies and becoming an honorary mother hero with a pension for life. Of course, not everybody was able to physically deliver that many babies. It was strange to see mothers with children ten to sixteen years apart. Financial incentives were so generous that women tried to get pregnant in middle age and were successful. It did not always bode well for the baby.

From the time a woman became pregnant, she stayed home pretending to be sick, on constant maternity leave. After the baby was born, mysterious illnesses plagued him/her until kindergarten. It was easy to obtain bogus baby illness certificates from doctors who barely survived themselves and relied on bribes from patients for their existence. Employers knew these medical certificates to be misrepresentations; nobody seemed to care, so long as everybody else received their meager monthly pay from the government. The work ethic mantra was, "they pretend to pay us, and we pretend to work."

A package of Kent cigarettes could buy a person sick with a cold or the flu three weeks of paid leave. A bar of foreign made Lux soap or a bottle of Nivea shampoo helped you see a doctor immediately as opposed to waiting weeks. A package of Chesterfield cigarettes might persuade the lab tech to do a chest X-ray the same day or a blood test in one week as opposed to months.

A cassette player would assure attentive health care from your government-assigned physician for a year. These doctors, who were told where to practice medicine, how many patients they had to see daily, and how much money they could earn, were so overwhelmed that the care they provided was substandard at best. They supplemented their meager incomes with bribes all the time, Hippocratic Oath notwithstanding.

These cons were not unlike the Pigford Settlement in which 88,000 farmers claimed that they have been discriminated against and denied the right to farm based on their skin color, each collecting $50,000 from the federal government. This is an obvious fraud since there are only around 40,000 farmers in the U.S.

I guess the argument could be made that people living under communism had no choice or opportunities to do anything else, whereas Americans are still free to pursue any American dream the honest way, starting from scratch, earning, and keeping the fruits of their labor, without expectation of "spreading the wealth around," a.k.a. welfare.

If an honest Romanian citizen tried to protest and reveal the labor dishonesty, he/she was quickly bribed, beaten, forced to shut up, or threatened by the communist syndicate or union.

There were honest people who tried to survive on their pay but they were very poor and needy, their existence quite precarious. The government did not care and it certainly did not honor the communist promise of "from each according to his ability, to each according to his needs." They had little food, lacked modern conveniences, education, and access to basic medical care. They were depressed, abusive and abused, often alcoholics, falling through the cracks of the communist workers' "paradise."

WHAT ARE YOUR ACCOMPLISHMENTS WORTH?

As any young person, I had dreams of grandeur for various professional careers. They changed on a whim, as often as the wind, with no particular rhyme or reason.

I wanted to be a famous actress, a famous writer, and an exceptional doctor who could save lives through groundbreaking procedures. I entertained the idea of being an engineer with the ability to build the ultimate machine that would allow humans to travel back in time. I wanted to find a cure for cancer, to be an accomplished painter, a violin player like my cousin, and even a gypsy vendor for a day so I could sell and eat all the sunflowers I wanted. The sky was the limit, but I always returned to my favorite game, playing teacher with my childhood friends.

If you ask me if my wild dreams came true, the answer is no. Did I continue playing teacher for almost thirty years, the answer is yes. Was it really a play? It might as well have been because I enjoyed teaching so much. Time flew, springs turned into winters; scores of wonderful students kept me young, challenged me in so many ways, and gave me the purpose to leave a small imprint into their futures. As a famous person said, teachers "touch the future. "I am not sure all students remember me with fondness or remember me at all, but some still do.

It was not easy being conservative among liberal colleagues. I had a few friends I cherished and even fewer who could truly understand where I came from and what life and education was like under communist regimes. We were mostly collegial and pretended to like one another. I never liked their views and they hated mine. They could not relate to someone coming from such a different culture and such a life of hardship.

One particular teacher stood out, she was brash, entertaining, and the darling of the teacher's union. She attended most conferences that the rest of us only dreamed of and was the automatic recipient of any award that a teacher could earn in their careers. By the end of her life, she had walls of "I love myself plaques" and ribbons given by various organizations under educational auspices.

Everything pedagogical she tried, right or wrong, silly or serious methodology of teaching was magical in the eyes of the administrators. She tested every fad and trend coming out of the State Department or College of Education "scholarly research."

After her funeral, her children put the house up for sale and personal belongings were disposed of or sold. To my surprise, there was a large barrel outside the house, on the curb, heaving full of my former colleague's awards, diplomas, and trophies.

I realized then with sadness that we are a mere blip in educational history, immediately forgotten after we pass on even by our very own children. I shed a tear for her devotion to her students and her children, devotion that ended in a trash bin. I am glad, she did not know how little these people really cared about her effort to make them understand that knowledge is power, to bring light into the darkness of the mind.

I picked up the contents of the barrel, piece by piece, and brought it to the school where she had spent most of her life teaching. I am not sure what they did with it, I hope it became part of that school's memorabilia.

When I retired, after having worked for twenty years for the same educational institution, the local liberal newspaper whose owners had a monopoly on all mass media, refused to print a small announcement of my retirement because my political views were known and diametrically opposed to their communist, Cuba loving, anti-American "values."

As Goethe is reputed to have said on his deathbed, "Licht, mehr Licht," light more light, our duty as teachers was to brighten the minds of young and old alike. Have we succeeded? You be the judge.

Personally, I still remember my middle school language and mathematics teachers. They left me with a lifelong love for language and for scientific reasoning. I can still see their faces, how they dressed, and their favorite expressions. They live on in my mind's eye. The knowledge they imparted is still valid and useful today.

I hope I have made such a lasting impression. I have wonderful memories of my students, our trips abroad, cultural stories, videos, and thousands of interesting and inspiring lessons and discussions we have had, but I am hard pressed to produce too many plaques and diplomas saying how wonderful of a teacher I was. They would not be worth much anyway if my children would throw them out with the garbage upon my departure from this world.

Everything in school, schedules, curriculum, research, travel, awards, recognition, materials, teaching environment, committees, revolved around popularity, politics, gifts, and brown-nosing. I despised such blatant disregard for professionalism and objectivity. I always believed in meritocracy and evaluation of worth based on student performance.

THIRTY YEARS OF FUN

It is hard to believe that I spent thirty years doing what I enjoyed most - teaching. I have done this many times for free - it came so easy to me and I felt that I owed back to society my expertise and the experience I had gained through many years of education both in Europe and the United States, living and traveling overseas. I spent twenty-five years as a full-time teacher and five years as a private teacher and graduate teaching assistant.

I remember playtime always involved me as the teacher, while my friends had to be dutiful students. There was no time in my mind that I contemplated very seriously doing something else.

I remember the trepidation of the first day of school, entering the classroom and seeing the anxious eyes of my students, wondering who is going to be the class clown, the brilliant but quiet student, the brown-noser, the know-it-all, the Goth, the shy, cannot-fit-in, the non-conformist, the loud-mouth, the creative, and the beauty queen who excelled at being popular.

My reputation preceded me, one generation of students told the other about the Romanian teacher who spoke 14 languages. It seemed that every year, the number of languages increased with my fame. I started with six and it had reached 14.

Meeting with parents twice a year on Parents and Orientation Day was also a whirlwind of fun since there were anxious expectations on both sides. I knew I would do my job in an exceptional way but I had to reassure the parents that their children will receive world-class education, unlike any institution they attended before. None of the teachers were unionized, most of them had Ph.D.s and considered teaching a vocation and their life's calling.

As a perfectionist, I did not want to teach unless I did it to perfection, unless I went far beyond the call of duty. No matter how much I was paid, my salary was never enough to compensate for the long hours and effort I put in to prepare my lessons and my delivery. I was always on a stage, giving 150%, whether it was 8 a.m. or 8 p.m., whether I felt poorly or terribly, my students deserved and got the best.

I went to great lengths to research a difficult question or to bring up-to-date information. I was the first teacher in the country to reach students in rural areas in the south via a fully interactive, fiber optic network supplied by Bellsouth in 1990. It was experimental, it was fun, and it was challenging.

I had regrets and cried often that I could not spend more time with my children as they grew up so fast. I brought them with me into the classroom all the time. Since first grade, they were a fixture in the back of my classroom, doing their homework, rolling their eyes at Mom's delivery and antics, after all, I was Mom, I could not seriously be a teacher, a teacher is a goddess on a pedestal, and I was just "Mom." How could I be anything else?

I allowed students to be themselves within certain understood parameters of classroom behavior. I allowed them to think, be creative, and express opinions in a non-threatening environment, while respecting the views of others. We traveled to far-away places and brought lessons back that were forever etched in their memories.

Some of the names have faded from my memory but their faces are still in my mind's eye. I have photographs of every class I have taught and, as I look at pictures of what some of my students have become, it is hard to match the high school or college photo with the adult of today.

I associate some students with minor mishaps such as accidentally shining a laser beam in the teacher's eye and blinding her for four days with minor permanent damage to one eye, special clothing they wore, hilarious hairdos, projects they completed, trips they took during which time they've gotten lost in a foreign country, winter formals, Tales from the Crypt, and Depression Day.

My students kept me young, smiling, laughing, and eager to go to work every day even though I disliked my progressive colleagues. They indoctrinated pupils every day into the vile communism that I had escaped in 1978. I closed my eyes and focused on the positive aspect of the job, teaching young minds to become proud and productive Americans.

Most of my students were naive idealists, socialists and communists at heart, wearing Che Guevara t-shirts, not really understanding the reality of what they believed in and advertised.

My former high school and college students are now productive members of society, with families, responsibilities, and I am proud that I was a tiny part of what they have become today, I am in essence "touching the future," even though I have retired from teaching.

SOCIAL ENGINEERING

Government dictated land use under the guise of sustainable development, sustainable communities, and social engineering are seemingly innocuous euphemisms. The reality is much more sinister, it is communist control of land use, agriculture, and housing.

I see in my mind's eye the grey landscape of drab and dirty concrete apartment complexes, crowded on the periphery of towns, close to polluting refineries, black smoke spewing steel factories, chemical plants, and other noxious industrial platforms.

The occupants of the small, one bedroom, one dining room, one bathroom, and one tiny kitchen apartments, had been living in villages surrounding large cities.

People had been forcefully moved so that the land they had previously occupied and owned could be confiscated, controlled, and farmed by the government for the "good of the people."

It was learned soon enough that the "good of the people" did not really exist; it was just a euphemism to enslave everyone to the communist party platform and its "caring" for the downtrodden.

A few villages escaped this social engineering because they were either too remote for practical mass agriculture or too scattered across the hills and mountains.

Such was the case of my paternal grandmother's village, perched high up in the Carpathian Mountains, a rocky but rich soil. Scattered patches of land allowed the locals to grow grapes and fruits, undisturbed by the confiscatory land grab of the communist party.

Farmers were able to make wine, jams, preserves, sell fresh fruit, while keeping all income. Being so isolated from the beaten path and being connected to the world by one weekly bus run, made it impossible and impractical for communist revenuers to come claim their lion's share for the "good of the people."

The neighborhoods that had been developed by the government "largesse" on the outskirts of towns were very poor and a sorry excuse for city living. Some did not have paved roads, running water, plumbing, or electricity. The mayor did not care about their fate although it was his job.

Over time, buildings decayed from lack of maintenance, updating, painting, roofing, earthquake damage, were eventually demolished or left abandoned just like a ghetto area in the U.S.

Row houses separated by wooden fences looked respectable on the outside but were not connected to any modern conveniences and lacked bathrooms on the inside. A wooden shack, the outhouse, loomed very smelly in the back.

The apartment blocks fared a little better because they had electricity, water, sewage, and garbage pickup when the government provided them. The problem was that the government could shut them off any time it wished, without prior notification. This included water, hot water, steam heat, electricity, and garbage pickup.

People had to maintain everything, clean, and provide security. Many blocks turned into ghetto areas, best to be avoided. Some became really dilapidated especially if occupied by gypsies who stripped them down and sold all interiors for spare parts, then abandoned them. What was the law going to do? There were not enough jails for all recidivists. Besides, gypsies could come and go as they pleased, they were feared by everyone.

Before the arrival of the communists to power, people had bucolic life styles, sufficient food, homes they called their own, a small plot of land, which they farmed and produced enough food on for their families and extra for the city market.

Communist social engineering changed that - most became poor, needy, hungry, cold, homeless, landless, and certainly lacking their human dignity as they became totally dependent on the government for all their needs. Nobody would own much of anything; everybody had to rent from the government.

If, in your American naiveté, are ever persuaded to even think that social engineering is a concept worthy of discussion, consider this - it is a communist code word for mass poverty and government dependency in perpetuity. Don't take my word for it, study history and review the same failed experiments in Cuba, formerly Iron Curtain countries of Eastern Europe, North Korea, and China, to name a few.

You can even take a short trip to Cuba to see the blight and dilapidation of formerly beautiful homes.

So many inhabited buildings in Havana are in such bad shape that even Roman ruins like the Coliseum, are better preserved. The buildings that would be condemned in this country were "socially engineered" and fundamentally destroyed by Fidel Castro's communist regime.

Cubans owned homes, hotels, and land before it was confiscated through clever rhetoric, finally by force, and distributed as rental property to the "proletariat." All fell in a sorry state of disrepair and remain that way to this day.

Bucolic life in the village (www.mycountry.ro)

Cart with oxen in Maramures (www.mycountry.ro)

WHY HAS COMMUNISM FAILED?

The last three years have been quite scary for me as I relived many things that I thought I left behind in communist Romania when I decided to immigrate to the United States in 1978.

I have déjà vus every day. I wake up wondering what freedoms have I lost today completely, have been curtailed, or are in the process of being curtailed through laws that none of the Congressmen who voted for them have read. How much closer am I today to living in a totalitarian society?

I wondered to myself, "What happened to the separation of powers" and to the famous American "checks and balances?" What happened to the rule of law and equal under the law that Americans were so famous for?

People shrug their shoulders, give me puzzled looks and cannot answer my questions. Everybody is putting his or her hopes on November's election and its outcome. What if the election does not turn the way we hope it will? What then? Are we going to be content to live under communism? International law? One world government?

These third world countries running the United Nations who desire and push for such one world government can barely run their own countries without a hefty handout and financial support from the United States. They are corrupt, fraught with civil and religious wars.

Are we going to trust our future and fortune to a corrupt world government that hates America and everything that we stand for, who is biting the hand that feeds them and protects them from wars, harm and natural disasters?

Why is it that we support corrupt governments that vote against the U.S. most of the time at the United Nations, yet we give them billions of dollars in aid and loans every year?

I used to think Romanians were so fortunate because they did not know how unfortunately poor and miserable they were in their daily lives. Now I think how unfortunate it is that Americans do not know how fortunate they are to live in the world's best country. They do not appreciate for a moment what God has given them through the luck of their birth.

Are we going to be able to sustain our superpower status? Are we going to be able to keep our freedoms? It does not seem so lately.

I do not take my freedoms as a naturalized American citizen for granted. I thank God every day that he gave me the opportunity to immigrate to this heaven called U.S.A. where I could become what I wanted if I was only willing to work hard, learn, and seize the opportunity to become a better person every day, unencumbered by total government control. "Carpe diem," said the Romans, "seize the day," I could do so because America had freedoms.

I am still in awe that I can make an appointment in a timely manner with a wonderfully trained doctor who cares and is willing to listen to my aches and pains, is bound by the Hippocratic Oath and values human life.

I can go to an Emergency Room anywhere in the country and I am treated within a reasonable amount of time even though I may or may not have insurance. There is an ambulance that will come if needed, even a helicopter.

Ambulances were a joke under communism. They came with no staff, no emergency equipment of any kind, and arrived not just hours later but days. There were drivers who would stop on the way to the hospital to pick up hitchhikers in order to make extra money. If the patient had days to live from God, he/she would survive through the medical neglect and potholes on the way to the hospital. Often the ambulance drove straight to the morgue.

I do not take for granted the fact the I can buy drugs that can ease my pain, cure my illness, or treat my symptoms. I still remember the pain as a teenager having root canal without anesthesia, blood spilling everywhere, screams of pain, while the dentist talked to his nurse and spat in my mouth. After five months of such torture, the tooth was pulled anyway. The root canal cost me nothing, but I got nothing but pain and torture.

Drugs were free, sort of, but the pharmacy shelves were always empty. I could bribe the pharmacist or buy them on the black market, if I had enough money. Black market prices for drugs were high if the low wages were considered.

The communist elites decided how much each profession could earn. Doctors, lawyers, teachers, professors, engineers made lower salaries than mechanics or miners.

Farmers survived on next to nothing. Their lands had been confiscated and the communist co-operative decided how much grain they could get after they worked all year long

Everywhere we went, we were herded like cattle, just another face and number in the crowd People were mean, impolite, and cruel to each other, impatient not because they did not have a heart, life was so hard that it toughened them and took away their humanity and kindness.

Medical vaccinations in schools were done with the same three syringes and needles, boiled every morning in a rusty pan, not autoclaved. What saved me from Hepatitis and other blood born diseases was the fact that my last name started with A and therefore I was the first one to receive such injections.

Polyclinics and hospitals used the same boiling practices, washed and re-washed bandages, gauze, and cotton. Patients' families had to provide food, sheets, and nursing care to their sick ones while in the hospital. Doctors would send them on the black market to buy medicines in order to treat the patient as the hospital pharmacy had ran out of drugs and money to purchase them. Rationing was the way the communist government offered FREE care to everyone.

I have lost many family members to medical malpractice, lack of care, lack of drugs, gross medical negligence, and rationing of care based on age or lack of connections to the elites in power.

People lingered for weeks in hospitals, ignored by medical staff, untreated, unfed, literally screaming in pain amidst wards of 30 beds lined up against the dirty walls, with no drugs available unless doctors and nurses were bribed.

We define civilization by our humanity. There was no humanity under communism. Life was worthless unless it was the life of those in power.

A baby born with a slight handicap was left to die unattended and incinerated. Communists had no time or money for imperfect human beings, they were expendable. They also ignored and mistreated the elderly. It was a family's duty to care for the elderly.

Communism did not just fail socially and medically, they also failed economically. We always carried a shopping bag with us and lots of extra cash. There were no credit cards or checks. The one Central Bank did not allow checking accounts, only savings and withdrawals from savings.

We had lots of cash on hand because we never knew when we might walk by a huge line, wrapping around for endless blocks, selling something. We never knew that the store was selling, but because the line was so huge, we knew, whatever it was, we needed it.

There were chronic shortages of everything because planning was done centrally by the communist apparatchiks who pretended to know what Economics was. Most of them were not educated at all; they were crass ideologues who carried the communist party line.

We were issued rationing coupons (looking like little stamps) for flour, cooking oil, sugar, butter, milk, and other staples. We could only eat vegetables and fruits in season. I will never forget my first trip to the American grocery store in January 1978! It was filled to the brim with every imaginable food that I had dreamed of when I was really hungry in Romania.

I remember being six years old and standing in line with my Mom at 4 a.m. in frigid weather to buy one liter of milk, butter, and sour cream. Sometimes, when the store opened at 6 a.m., we were told that only 30 people in line would be lucky enough to buy that day because that is all the truck had brought in that morning. The rest of us had to go home empty-handed.

We did not buy milk to drink, we reserved it for babies, or for cooking. It was a luxury to have a hot cup of cocoa with milk. We could not even buy vitamins in order to supplement the lack of calcium in the diet. Vitamins were hard to find, only available if you got sick. Even then, the shelves were often empty.

The communist system failed us judicially. The justice system only favored the people in power; it was us, the proletariat, the unwashed masses, against the ruling communist elite. We had no due process; we were guilty until proven innocent. And the police was not there to protect us but to harass us.

The communist system did not allow us to pray to God, believe in God, own a Bible, or have Bible studies in the home. It was against the law! Only in marriage, baptism, and death were we allowed to go to church. Funeral homes did not exist so churches were the logical places for last rites.

Communists failed to recognize private ownership. Nobody was allowed to own anything in excess of what they made and people were encouraged to snitch on each other and even paid extra to do so.

The population was tightly controlled economically. Freedom to move from job to job, from town to town was highly discouraged. Any citizen had to report within a week any move whether permanent or temporary.

Foreign visitors were not allowed in a private home as they were considered potential spies and thus we would be collaborating with the enemy. Housing such foreigners would be punished by jail time.

Traveling was discouraged. If a visa was issued, few people could afford the travel expenses and the rest of the family was held hostage on the promise of jail time if their family member did not return from the trip. My dad was jailed and beaten up many times when my mom chose to remain in the U.S. He eventually succumbed to such beatings and maltreatment on May 12, 1989.

It is alleged that the Dictator Nicolae Ceausescu's family engaged in fiscal and moral debauchery at the expense of the Romanian people and especially the young. Nicu, his youngest son, was famous for his Roman style parties at the Intercontinental Hotel. He had his choice of girls, kidnapped by the Security Police assigned to him and forcefully brought to the party. He drank so much that he often urinated onto plates of food in view of everyone present. He died years later, after the fall of communism, from severe liver failure.

The country's treasury was his for the taking. Millions of dollars earmarked for economic development were deposited into Swiss Bank accounts in their names.

Communists confiscated our guns in the middle of the night under the guise of safety. They confiscated our land, paintings, furniture, cars, stores, money saved, gold, jewelry, anything of value under the guise of collectivization and fair distribution of wealth. People who had more accumulated wealth had to go to jail in addition to having their wealth confiscated because they were bourgeois. One of my uncles served 7 years in jail for having too many houses and a store. He survived the 7 years of hard labor but was very ill for many years afterwards from the lack of proper care and nutrition.

We had the right and obligation to vote but there was only one candidate on the ballot. They came and got us from home and watched over our shoulders while we filled the ballot. The voting records were always 100% for the communist party. Who wanted to go to jail?

Life was very hard; we had chronic shortages of electricity, water, and heat. Few people owned a TV or refrigerator. Our refrigerator was the windowsill in wintertime. Birds learned really fast and made frequent raids on our handy outdoor storage.

If we needed 1 million pairs of black boots for winter, the centralized government, without any forethought, would deliver only 50,000 pairs of white boots and a battle and bribery would ensue over these boots. People were so demoralized, "they pretended to work and the government pretended to pay them."

That was the communist work ethic. A barter exchange of stolen goods from the work place developed as a tool of survival. A butcher shop worker would steal meat to trade for milk with the worker from the dairy.

I think I have made my point that communism is a disaster on every societal level and a failure in every country that has tried it. Even the few remaining communist countries are now beginning to move away from this failed model, yet the United States is charging full steam ahead in the direction of the proverbial iceberg that will sink the Titanic.

My question and challenge to us is, are we going to allow it to happen? Are we going to allow the destruction of our 235-year-old republic, the most successful country on the planet on an empty promise from a didactic and ideological administration?

What would our Founding Fathers say today? What would all the heroes say, who have sacrificed their lives so that we may live free? We owe it to our children and grandchildren to leave the republic better than we have found it, not worse.

Ileana in 2nd grade as young pioneer (first on right)

AN AMERICAN BY CHOICE

Why did I decide to move to the U.S. and become an American citizen? Because I wanted to be free! I wanted to have children and a family in the freest republic in the world, the shining city on the hill.

I can still see my Dad hunched over our huge short wave radio broadcasting Voice of America, a glimmer of hope in his eyes that someday freedom would arrive in our home. He always gave me a wink as if to say, do not worry, we have a secret pact, we will succeed, and God is on our side.

I was stripped of my rights simply because I wanted to live in the U.S.A., land of the free, home of the brave. Americans have no appreciation for their citizenship by birth, at least not until they are in danger of losing it.

I was so elated to be free, I was ready to kiss the frozen ground when I landed in New York. I was so penniless, I could not even afford a soda or a phone call, but I was finally free!

The Romanians had rejected me but Americans (well, some of them) were embracing me. I had to earn the rights, privileges, responsibilities, and the honor bestowed upon American citizens.

I respected and saluted the American flag for giving me and millions of other immigrants freedom from oppression. I knew what totalitarian control was.

I had to learn idiomatic expressions. I did not demand that everything be translated into Romanian for me or press 2 for Romanian.

I paid to have my babies delivered in a hospital and did not expect free medical care or demand it. I made monthly payments for years to the local hospital until the bills were paid.

I taught my daughters both English and Romanian and, as they grew older, they appreciated the bilingualism, their Romanian roots, but they were Americans first and foremost.

After two years of being a legal resident alien, an immigration officer in Memphis interrogated me why I belonged to the young pioneers, the precursor to the Communist Party. In a communist society, indoctrination started in pre-school whether parents agreed to it or not. I had to speak English well, could not show up with a translator for the citizenship test or the swear-in ceremony as they do today for Spanish-speaking applicants.

I was approved and sworn in as a Naturalized Citizen of the United States of America. It was a proud day for me and almost eight years in coming. My Dad's spirit was with me and my Mom and daughter were in the audience. I was no longer "persona-non-grata," I had gained a country, a language, safe borders, and country resplendent with a tapestry of many nations, ethnicities, all united by a common language and goal, freedom. We were truly a melting pot, not a tossed salad bowl.

I do not take my citizenship lightly and I abhor the burning of our flag. I get tears of pride and joy when the National Anthem is played and the Pledge of Allegiance is recited.

I respect all legal immigrants just like me who are waiting their turn patiently, filling out forms after forms, waiting years sometimes to receive or be denied a visa to freedom. Vast oceans separate them from our borders. Does that make them less deserving of becoming legal residents of the U.S. because they are not able to jump a fence or swim across the Rio Grande?

Illegal aliens are law-breakers; they are not "undocumented citizens living in the shadows," or "new citizens," the euphemisms that liberals keep supplying to justify an illegal act that should be punished according to the law of the United States. As a very smart radio personality, Michael Savage, once said, we are defined by our "borders, language, and culture." If we do not defend our borders, we cease to be a nation, we become a lawless land.

May 20, 1982 was for me the day when the vast ocean that separated Europe from the United States no longer existed and I became a free American citizen by choice.

PC IN LIFE

I always found politics boring. I am a typical American who loathes the deceptiveness and hypocrisy of Washington. If a person fails at anything else, he/she can still go into politics. It does not require a high I.Q., college education, or a blue blood background - just street smarts, cunning, a lot of money, donated through legal or illegal means, perhaps a vast personal fortune, and the ability to persuade voters that he/she is the best candidate for ANY job, even a snow job.

An honest, poor individual stands a very slim chance at making it in public "service." I never understand why it is called service since nobody really serves its constituents once in office, only their own interests and the advancement of their careers.

Politics has a price directly related to the self-importance of the politician and the hierarchy of public office. Morally speaking, the price of politics is sometimes one's lost soul.

It is hard to stomach politicians dodge questions artfully, while deceiving and covering illegal deeds and shady shenanigans. To an outsider, it looks like all politicians attend the same grooming school of artful dodging, misrepresentation, and purposeful deception via ridiculous rhetorical euphemisms and seldom fulfilled promises.

It is so painful to watch politicians lie, cheat, claw, and steal their supremacy to seats of power, leveraging friends, family, acquaintances, and fortunes for the chance to make a pact with the devil. With such representation, will my country survive? Will it still be a beacon of light, liberty, justice, and opportunity for all? Will it still be the shining city on the hill? Will we still be proud to call ourselves the caretakers of the world? There was a sign of pride and joy when people were saying, "the Americans are coming to save us, don't worry." We were the last bastion of justice for the oppressed. We always defended and protected the citizens and the people with no voice of their own.

Politicians do not mind throwing their parents, wives, and children under the bus if it helps them gain a few votes. A secret handshake, an empty promise, a check pressed against sweaty palms during a handshake, a free golf trip in an exotic location, perks a la Nancy Pelosi on the government or privately owned luxury jets, jaunts in exotic locations, buyouts, financial swaps, all in the name of representing the downtrodden who have a hard time finding or keeping a job, feeding their children, and keeping their homes.

Politicians tend to deliver on promises to the very poor by offering them a nanny existence from cradle to grave, assuring perpetual poverty and dependence on the mighty government who, through its largesse, enslaved them in perpetuity for a measly vote. This vote will always be there, even after they passed away. Generations of Democrats create a tradition of poverty in the slums.

Everything in life IS political: education, religion, military, employment, government, medicine, clubs, housing, marriage, family, etc. It starts before a child is old enough to talk - parents manipulate the system to make sure their progeny is accepted in the best day care and pre-school. God forbid they should attend public schools, they are doomed!

Admission to Ivy League schools is often based on a family's tradition of attendance; the student might be weaker, but the family's blue blood past and financial contributions to the alumni fund are stellar.

Preferences are even given to minorities over better-qualified and scored students. Quotas and Affirmative Action are political methods of leveling the playing field and soothe the conscience of the trust-funded. After all, it is "social justice," a code word for communism. Politics is thus controlling who can and cannot attend institutions of higher learning. As the government has taken over student loans, the control over university attendance will become more and more politicized, to the disadvantage of the more conservative students. Preference will be given to liberal students and to those who are registered Democrats or contribute heavily to Democratic causes.

Hiring and tenure of faculty is political - liberals are always promoted first, the darlings of the administration; conservatives are often denied tenure. Spouses of sought-after professors are hired over much better prepared applicants.

Union hacks and College of Education ideologues with thin resumes and easy degrees such as Sociology, Psychology, Social Work, and Women's Studies are the darlings of the conference circuit and professorial committees.

The more controversial and outrageous a professor's class, the more beloved, prestigious, and higher salaried they became.

Graduate school teaching assistantships tend to go to foreigners, particularly in science where the language barrier creates a problem for tuition paying Americans who expect clear and precise English language delivery of lectures. It is expected politically to favor those who are here illegally and are sub-standard students. Their mere presence expiates all the perceived wrongs committed in the past by previous generations of Americans against poor, unfortunate souls, whoever they may be. The responsibility of such wrongs does not have an expiration date; each new generation of Americans must be made financially responsible for the sins of the past.

Religion is particularly difficult to climb into the ranks of power. The politics are evil, corrupt, and downright mean. Members of a congregation can cause hurt and pain to many people during the week, yet pretend to be good and pray on weekends. Somehow, all the sins of the week are washed away by the goodness of attending church on Sunday and filling the coffers of the church. Teenage and out of wedlock motherhood are praised in church, celebrated, and encouraged in the name of political correctness.

Military members rise to the ranks of power through family tradition, quota system, affirmative action, nepotism, manipulation, protégé status, and dirty maneuvering. PC has put in danger the lives of many a soldiers, yet few are complaining in the halls of power. Complain and your career is dead.

Employment is seldom based on merit. Connections, luck, education, experience, nepotism, personality traits, talent or lack thereof, being in the right place at the right time, good looks, dressing well are some of the variables that come into play when successfully gaining employment. Being deceptive, blackmailing, using sex as a weapon, bribery, cheating on tests, are acceptable political maneuvers to get a desired job.

A hospital is a microcosm of politicians vying for a larger slice of the political pie - better working conditions, better pay, better benefits, sex with doctors and nurses, access to drugs, no accountability when life and death mistakes are made, perks to exotic locations conferences, and yearly promotions.

How many times are politicians held responsible down the road, years after they have exited public office, for the disastrous policies they have voted for, which have impoverished and destroyed the lives of many generations of Americans? Unsuspecting Americans pay the price of fiscal slavery without knowing why.

How many doctors are held responsible or even care what happens to their patients once they leave the hospital? Yes, we have lawyers, but try to sue a doctor for malpractice and see how successful you are. The politics of legal precedent get in the way.

The competition for government positions is cutthroat but less visible than the fight for a political post. Politicians fight in full public view - their laundry is aired every day and skeletons uncovered, unless they are the darlings of the communist media, in that case, they can do no wrong, everything is glossed over or ignored. In government, careers can literally be made or destroyed overnight with one mistaken decision. Employees use the media to advance their agendas the same way politicians and actors do but less visibly.

Club membership is very political and elitist at the same time. Even presidents or heads of state can be denied membership in such rarefied environments. The name of Ronald Reagan comes to mind, he was denied membership in a prestigious golf club.

Private clubs can certainly deny access to anybody they wish without really stating a reason for such denial. Using huge annual fees that are prohibitive to most people is another way in which "undesirables" are kept away. Public clubs cannot exclude people, at least on the surface.

Housing is political as well. Home Owner Associations have complex rules of residence, behavior, maintenance, expensive fees, and arcane rules and regulations, which can exclude many people. Political boards can refuse any person they wish to keep away from their neighborhood. Even flying the American flag can rub a resident alien the wrong way and it has to disappear.

We no longer cater to the majority but to a very strange, leftist minority with an anti-American agenda. I am not sure, when the switch occurred, but it is here to stay, like the tentacles of an octopus that embeds each razor sharp tooth into the skin of the nation.

The politics of family are as varied as are the families in the U.S. Everybody has a strange aunt, a weird parent, an estranged wild child, a libidinous cousin, a curmudgeon grandparent, and a favorite or disliked yearly event that they must attend in order to keep peace and harmony.

We cannot pick and choose who our relatives are or how they behave publicly and privately. We love to hate them or hate to see them even once a year; it takes a lot of strength to pretend otherwise. Publicly, they are the best relatives or the best family on the planet. And that is political astuteness to lie with a straight and confident face.

Marriage is more difficult to describe as politics, but it is. It is a contract between two people who know full well they are going to violate it at some point, yet they go ahead and swear on the proverbial Bible that they will represent the will of the people, in this case, the two married people, until Death do them part.

Justice is a political sport, opponents jousting for the truth yet employing only half-truths in the process, bogus science, manipulated statistics, false testimony, and fake court briefs or "amicus curiae." Judges are very much political appointees or politically elected. Justice is no longer blind and no longer balanced. Justice has rose-colored glasses.

According to William Lind, political correctness is similar to Marxism because they are both totalitarian ideologies that allow no dissent. All history is determined by power, nothing else matters. Certain groups of people are good, such as feminist women, blacks, Hispanics, and homosexuals. These same groups of people are considered victims. White males are evil. Expropriation is a way to return to the government what was stolen from them. ("Elements of Political Correctness")

How much further are we going to take political correctness? As long as people are afraid to confront those from the left who promote and make a living from victimhood, the advance of PC is likely to continue. Churches are next.

1966 currency in circulation in 1978

HOW MUCH IS 32,000 LEI WORTH?

My parents have worked very hard their entire lives. Every penny they could save beyond the daily expenses to survive went into a savings account towards the purchase of their own home.

The ultimate dream was home ownership that few could afford before the age of retirement. Purchases were made with cash and it took that many years to build enough savings to attempt acquisition of a one or two bedroom apartment. Anything larger was considered lavish and bourgeois, frowned upon and investigated by the Economic Police.

An arbitrary presidential decree, similar to an executive order here in the U.S., excluded, of course, the ruling elite and their families. They resided in and "owned" the homes taken by government decree from their previous owners who were declared "enemies of the people," simply because they owned a larger home or more than one piece of real estate.

An urban home was a bit of a stretch since most Romanians were crowded into grey and drab concrete block apartments built in haste by the communist government, scrambling to create a socialist society on its way to communist utopia.

Many such apartment blocks were crumbling shortly after completion because the concrete had not been properly mixed or was poured in wintertime in less than ideal engineering conditions. Answering to barely educated communist apparatchiks who only understood deadlines, not safety, pushed many builders to complete dwellings that were unsafe for human habitation. Decay and polluted buildings dotted the city landscape. No amount of green grass or flowers could cheer up the scene.

Country houses were much safer, built of bricks and wood, one-story homes with no indoor plumbing and with wooden outhouses. Some poorer ones were made of mud bricks, offering natural cooling in summertime and warmth in wintertime from wood burning stoves.

A very strong earthquake in March of 1977 demolished scores of such apartment buildings. Many crumbled into large piles of dust and steel bars. Some residents contributed to the problem by knocking out walls in order to enlarge their meager abodes. They did not realize that it weakened the support structure of the overall building.

My parents and I were lucky - the building survived with severe damage. This one-minute long earthquake, measuring over 7.2 on Richter Scale, left such large cracks in the walls that we could see the outside. Many months later, support beams in place, the building was repaired, however weakened the core may have been. We prayed and hoped that there would not be another strong earthquake any time soon.

There were always tremors, registering on the Richter Scale, it was part of life. We lived in earthquake alley. The Vrancea Mountains had a huge fault that was constantly active and heaving large plates against each other. We were used to chandeliers swaying, furniture sliding across the floors, and china and glassware breaking. Treetops will elegantly sway to the ground, sometimes snapping, as if a giant was caressing the rooftops.

As a long-time Southern resident in the U.S., if I had to choose now, I am not sure if I would pick the uncertainty of living with the possibility of earthquakes or the constant tornado warnings and occurrences.

I remember the early evening as if it was yesterday. I was taking a shower when the first rumble hit, the noise of a thousand thundering trains approaching. My daddy was banging on the door, yelling that I should run out of the building.

Everything seemed in slow motion, I was fascinated by the swaying and the cracking noise, the groans coming from the middle of the earth, staring at the walls, convinced that I was going to die, but my morbid curiosity wanted to know what my last seconds were going to be as the walls were beginning to split and door frames were coming apart.

I knew that I was not a fast runner. My chances of outrunning Mother Nature and Romanian construction were zero. We lived on the fifth floor of a building with no elevator. I decided to stay put in spite of my dad's yelling to get out.

I remember the weeks afterwards, having to walk past the two-story high piles of dust and steel left behind by thousands of many storied buildings that had collapsed, on my slow walk to school.

It was eerie, life was going on, and I could not understand how we could still have classes around so much devastation. And the smell of death! It was sad and numbing but gave us a purpose around so much sadness.

Nobody dared to stay indoors; we slept outside for weeks, under the stars, on the cold, grassy ground. Late March in Romania of 1977 was still pretty cold. Many aftershocks kept us running outside from buildings for months until the routine set in again.

After the building was repaired, the government decided that all the renters had to purchase their apartments or they had to move out. My family contemplated the possibility of homelessness as they had nowhere else to go, but vagrancy was against the law.

Our one-bedroom apartment had been arbitrarily priced at 30,000 lei. I say arbitrarily although the amount may have been directly tied to the cost per unit of the structure repairs done to the entire building after the earthquake. The government was broke and needed some way to recover expenses.

Under different conditions, I do not think anybody would have desired to purchase these basic, ugly apartments; they would have been satisfied with renting, as it was the case and still is for some Europeans.

The cost of owning a home is quite out of reach for most people. I never understood why Americans think that owning a home is a right, expect, and demand vociferously from their government the right to a free home. Communism does not give anybody a home for free!

The Romanian Central Bank (C.E.C.) put a hold on my parents' 32,000 lei savings account as future payment for the 30,000 lei apartment. The purchase date was set for 1989, eleven years later! Communists were never in a hurry to do anything, the bureaucracy was too cumbersome - phones and TV service took fourteen years, buying a car ten years, there were endless lists for every purchase and service. Prompt service with a smile was not part of the communist vocabulary.

My daddy passed away in May 1989, my mom defected to the U.S., and a revolution took place that replaced and executed the communist dictator Ceausescu in December 1989. Our apartment was never purchased and the money remained in escrow, controlled by the new government. To add insult to injury, every personal possession, from photographs, furniture, clothes, books, dishes to my parents' wedding painting were also confiscated. To this day, my mom is very bitter about the loss of her life's mementoes.

The newly installed government had no idea how to run a capitalist economy based on supply and demand, all they knew was communist economics based on the rotten ideas of Karl Marx, an indolent moocher who hated manual labor and chose to come up with ideas to confiscate wealth from others and spread it around in order to survive. He needed Frederich Engels, the son of a successful Prussian businessman, to subsidize his laziness and lack of desire to provide for his family. Karl Marx' wife and children went often hungry and cold, on a diet consisting of bread and potatoes.

As the newly appointed and then elected government began to print money out of control, without any backing by goods and services, the money supply became so large, there was too much money chasing too few goods. Inflation set in, followed by hyperinflation. My parents' 32,000 lei could now either purchase three loaves of bread or two pounds of meat.

When an old house was demolished recently to make room for a parking lot, the construction crew found a buried "damigeana," a very large, bottle shaped, glass container in a straw braided cage, filled with Ceausescu money, almost one million lei.

Under different circumstances, such a vessel would be used for home-made moonshine. Apparently, the owners of the house had buried the treasure for safekeeping. These one million lei was now worthless, as the transition to a new devalued currency had been made. It was a fortune under Ceausescu; it was now worth something only to numismatic collectors.

My parents worked very hard to save 32,000 lei to buy their dream home. This worthless dream is now accumulating interest in a bank somewhere in Romania, an account that nobody can claim or cash in.

Communist apartment blocks

FILL HER UP!

I pulled up to my corner gas station and noticed that the price of gas had inched up ten cents more. Every day the price goes up by a few cents. It is now over three dollars a gallon. I thank God I no longer own the Toyota that only accepted premium gasoline. If I tried to cheat and mix it with lower grades, it sputtered and jerked unhappily until it stopped.

I noticed the few Prius owners giving me superior looks of "I am saving the planet, why are you driving something else?" I am picturing the huge battery in the trunk of a hybrid that is very toxic and expensive to dispose of, actually causing more damage to the environment than my conventional exhaust spewing engine. Who thinks that a Prius is a nice-looking, muscle car?

I asked the gas station owner why his prices are going up every day. He tells me that there is a tacit collusion between owners; he would be chewed if he did not charge the same price as the other owners. As far as why he thinks gas is going up, he shrugs his shoulders and goes about his morning routine.

I am debating in my head the disastrous energy policies of the current administration, oil-drilling moratoriums, and all the phony green energy, and the jobs that were supposedly "created or saved."

I am thinking of OPEC and their overt collusive successful attempts of controlling oil prices and production. The 11-member Organization of Petroleum Exporting Countries has reduced production of oil times and times again in the interest of raising prices world-wide. In a sense, since they are producing 40% of the world's oil production, they have the power to control how we live and what we pay to fuel our economy.

OPEC is a cartel and economists in general view cartels as terrible forms of market organization as it is inefficient and flies in the face of consumer welfare. They control somewhat the price and certainly the flow of oil. History has shown that price controls on various commodities have caused painful shortages.

A war in 1973 between Israel and Arab nations caused OPEC to quadruple oil prices. Prices of raw materials shot through the roof while food prices increased as well in part due to poor harvests in various parts of the world. As energy became more expensive, businesses cut back, causing a reduction in productivity and thus a recession.

Things are never as simple as they seem because there are too many variables coming into play. If one adds enough variables, just about every economic theory proves to be wrong and so are the textbooks espousing them.

In 1933, President Franklin Roosevelt established that the U.S. would buy and sell gold at the constant rate of $35 per ounce. Officials at Bretton Woods conference in New Hampshire turned to the dollar as the basis for a new international economic order after World War II since the U.S. held the lion's share of the world's gold reserves.

When Richard Nixon ended in 1971 the dollar to gold convertibility, Pandora's box of ills was opened wide. The dollar had been fixed at $35 per gold ounce for a long time. Anybody knew how to convert foreign currencies on any given day into gold and into dollars. There was no fluctuation between currencies on a day by day basis. Money was always worth a certain amount of silver and gold and that never changed.

Nixon opened a huge can of worms, allowing politicians in Washington to print paper dollars out of thin air, without any backing by goods and services, thus causing inflation. And the out-of-control spending began.

Gold is a commodity in relative short supply as all the gold that was ever mined can fit into the cargo hold of a large petroleum tanker. We are not likely to find any huge reserves to be mined any time soon. Mining for gold is a very painstaking and expensive process as it takes the removal of tones of dirt and/or stone to harvest one ounce of gold. Gold prices go up and down, currently most up, in the stratosphere of $1,300 plus per ounce, but its worth as commodity money never changes. It is the value of the dollar with which gold is purchased that fluctuates wildly since the dollar is a currency deemed "worthy" by "fiat" by the American government. "Fiat" is a Latin term for "let it be." Otherwise the dollar is only worth the cotton/linen paper it is printed on and the labor and ink involved in printing it. The wild fluctuation in value has to do with the amount of currency in circulation and the faith and trust in American government and its investments.

How much confidence do Americans and foreign investors have right now in the American dollar? How much business confidence do Americans have? Why is everyone afraid to invest right now? How much consumer confidence do people in general have? The answer lies with the declining sales in every sector. Two-thirds of Gross Domestic Product is consumption.

The worth of a currency is determined by many factors such as inflation, demand for investment and goods in a specific country, interest rates in that country, just to name a few. The most interesting variable that makes a currency desirable or not desirable to have is the faith in the government of that country and the political stability of its government. We all know right now how much faith American people have in their own government, its policies, and its ability to run the country. If Americans don't trust their government, how worthy is the U.S. dollar? If public confidence sinks, the dollar devalues. This devaluation of the dollar by printing money without backing of goods and services is called inflation. And the Federal Reserve System, our central bank, is doing just that at the moment, in order to deal with the vast spending that the 111th Congress engaged in 2010. As a matter of fact, this Congress has spent more this year than all the previous 110 Congresses had.

Complicating the picture are petrodollars, or oil dollars. Petrodollars are U.S. dollars earned by a country from the sale of petroleum. The term was coined in 1973 by Ibrahim Oweiss, a professor at Georgetown University.

The Bretton Woods conference in New Hampshire established the dollar as the world's "reserve currency." This is a fly in the ointment because oil is bought all over the world using the U.S. dollar as an international currency, a global medium of exchange. OPEC keeps increasing the price of crude to guard themselves against future drops in the value of the U.S. dollar which is the international currency that oil trades in.

If the U.S. allows the free fall of the dollar by printing huge amounts to deal with its government out-of-control spending, OPEC sees its revenues plunge and has no other choice but to raise oil prices. Add to the problem the speculating on the Chicago Board of Trade of oil, currency, and gold commodities futures and you have a severe crisis.

Since gold is a reliable commodity, people are buying it in larger quantities, including oil rich Arabs who see their dollar holdings worth less, day by day, thanks to the American government's inept handling of the economy and out-of-control spending. Whether this is done on purpose to bankrupt our country, that is another issue.

After 1971, U.S. could buy crude oil for as little as $1 a barrel - now it is approaching $100 a barrel. Consumers could buy premium gas for as little as 28 cents a gallon in the early 70s. Gasoline is now approaching $4 a gallon in some states.

Unemployment figures are dire. Discouraged workers have stopped looking for work and are thus no longer counted. If we were to take into account millions of such workers, the figure would be much larger than the 9% reported by the Bureau of Labor Statistics. How many more people are going to lose their jobs as gasoline goes up and everything becomes more expensive?

Are we a self-sufficient nation that could drill its way out of this problem instead of shipping our wealth and prosperity to oil rich nations who wish as harm? The seven year moratorium on drilling in the U.S. imposed recently by the Obama administration certainly dooms our ability to become self-sufficient in oil production. Many nations such as China, Russia, Cuba, Vietnam, Venezuela, Brazil, to name just a few, are furiously buying oil leases and drilling in the Gulf of Mexico, right in our own back yards, exploiting our reserves while we are forbidden by our own government to drill.

There are rich oil shales that could be exploited as well, but environmentalists lobby Congress constantly to forbid drilling and exploration in their zealous attempt to either protect the environment or some endangered species of rodent, amphibian, bird, or fish. In the process, the interest of protecting humans becomes irrelevant as humans are seen as more expendable. According to environmentalists, there are almost 7 billion of us, and we are straining the resources of the planet. White House czars advise that population must be culled drastically in order to reduce the permanent damage we cause to the environment by our mere existence.

As we watch the price of oil escalate yet again, our economy and standard of living will suffer immeasurably, since crude oil is the engine that drives the energy behind our productivity. Our way of life and survivability are inexorably threatened.

Ileana Johnson Paugh

Village water well in 2010

CPSIA information can be obtained at www.ICGtesting.com
Printed in the USA
LVOW042146170412

278073LV00006B/159/P